MW00815332

'I THINK MY DAD WAS BORN IN A BARN'

VOLUME I

'My father's memories of everyone's childhood'

A compilation of witty short stories by my dad, Tony E. Windsor, from his weekly column featured in Morning Star Publications, Inc.

Compiled by

Aaron T. Windsor

I would like to dedicate this compilation of my father's short stories to the other half of my life's inspiration, my mother, Bea Truitt Bowman. Your courage and strength in the face of such great challenge is awe inspiring and I love you!

Aaron Windsor

Foreword

I think everyone regards their youth as somewhat magical; at least after they have experienced it and then become involved in the chaos of adulthood. My childhood was probably not much different than that of most other people my age.

When I was a child my father would always remind me that I was experiencing the greatest moments of my life. He would insist that at some point I would look back as an adult and wish I could somehow travel back in time and re-live these fleeting moments of youth. I listened to my father, but really didn't strive to hear his message. After all, it was my goal as a child to hurry up and get past this stage of my life and become an adult and experience that dream of independence.

Guess what? My father was right. I am now a 35-year-old man and all I seem to think about is my youth and how carefree my life was during those days. I actually find myself remembering those words from my father and longing for a time machine that would sweep me back to the days of my childhood and less independence.

I should have recognized something during my youth that I am very well aware of now as an adult; my father is an authority on the subject of nostalgia and dreams of yesterday. He invested a good portion of his working career taking other people on trips down his personal "Memory Lane."

My father is a writer. He has written two books and literally thousands of newspaper articles and weekly columns. It is his columns that I have recently become interested in. As a young boy I recall my father writing a weekly column in two community newspapers, most recently, the Seaford & Laurel Star newspapers, in western Sussex County, Delaware.

He wrote these columns at a time when I was old enough to read, but for some reason at that time they did not interest me. These weekly nostalgic reflections were simply part of what my Dad did for a job. I had little time to invest in anything other than my own daily explorations of youth.

Now, as an adult and father myself, I find great comfort in reading about how my father grew up and the things he did as a young boy growing up in Crisfield, Maryland. As I poured over the archive editions of the newspapers and took the long overdue trip down "Memory Lane," I realized something special. My father may have grown up in a different time and different place than me, but his childhood exploits reminded me so much of my own.

I recall vividly the many times that people twice my father's age would stop him in the grocery store, or at a community event, and tell him how much they felt his columns reflected their own personal childhood experiences and memories.

After reading my father's columns, some he had written as many as 25 years ago, I decided to make it a personal mission to bring some of these columns together and make them available to other people. These are by no means literary epics, but simply light-hearted, feel-good, writings. However, I have personally seen the excitement and joy that people have expressed when talking to my father about the most recent column they had read in the newspaper.

I have begged my father to compile a book based on his columns and his response has always been, "That would certainly be egotistical, now wouldn't it?" So, while I am not a writer, I am taking this job on as a labor of love. My father did the writing, now I just want everyone to join me in the reading; and the ride down Dad's "Memory Lane." I think you may find like I have, that the journey passes directly through your own childhood.

Aaron Windsor,
Tony Windsor's son

Photo top left is Aaron Windsor with his father, Tony (1980). The photo top right is Aaron with his grandfather, Tom Windsor (The Boss) in about 1981. In the photo left, Aaron asked his father to be his best man at his wedding in 2001.

Introduction

When my son said he wanted to gather up some of my weekly columns and put them in a book, my response was much like that which would come should someone suggest I build an elephant stable – "Why?"

I considered his idea, and while admirable and well-meaning, I told him this would certainly appear to many as akin to conceited and egotistical; two things that I have never been blessed to demonstrate with any degree of honesty or confidence.

His persistence and enthusiasm regarding the subject brought about the very results that his whining and begging did when he was a little boy harping on one of his many wants. I simply told him, "Do, it and leave me alone."

He actually did move forward and now here is a book. I am very proud and humbled that my son finds anything that I have done over the years worthy of sharing with others as a source of pride. When he was a young boy I always recall that he tried desperately to make sure I would not somehow appear near him and his friends and create great embarrassment.

I appreciate that he has taken the time to search the newspaper archives and pick out some of my columns that he finds enjoyable. To be honest, I never actually thought he read any of them.

These columns are far from literary genius and probably border on the ramblings of a simpleton. However, I am a nostalgic person and take great solace in revisiting my past. There seems to be little stress in days that have now gone by.

I must give utmost credit to God for blessing me with the opportunities I have had and helping me to write. I want to express appreciation to my mother (Frances) and late father (Tom) Windsor, and my siblings, Tom, Jeff, Rob, and Carol. They have allowed me to write in great detail about life around the Windsor house; although I suppose they had little option.

I also want to especially thank Bryant and Carol Richardson, owners of Morning Star Publications, Inc., who have afforded me the venue to write my columns and share my sometimes nonsensical thoughts of everyday life.

Lastly, but most importantly, I want to express great appreciation to those people who have taken the time to stop me in the grocery store, restaurant, or department store, to tell me that they have read and enjoyed my column. For these people to tell me that much of what I have written reminds them of their youth and growing up, leaves me extraordinarily humbled.

With that, I will simply say, let the reading begin!

Tony E. Windsor

The hazards of home

It occurs to me that as I recall my childhood home, I resided in less than a completely safe environment. It seems my family home was riddled with opportunities to break a leg or split a skull.

As kids, my brothers and I slept upstairs. A door in the living room led up to the stairs. At the top of the staircase was a less than stable banister that was our only barrier from a 20-foot drop to the base of the stairs below. Given that this banister was prone to sway at the slightest touch of the human hand, we obviously were very cautious whenever we walked past it; that is of course if we were the least bit civilized.

Like a bunch of African spider monkeys, each one of us had our own special way to walk up or down the stairs. We would ride the top of the banister like a mechanical bull and then grab the base of the banister and swing out over the open stairwell like a bunch of circus apes. There was never the slightest fear of injury; we were indestructible.

Though we were certainly guilty of putting our own safety in jeopardy, Mom was not completely innocent of contributing to the household hazards as well. Wall-to-wall carpeting was something that we only knew about through movies, or when we visited our great-aunt and uncle in Baltimore.

Today it is common place; even considered stylish to have hardwood floors. I know people who sand their floors down to the original wood just the get that old-fashion decorum for their rooms.

We had hardwood floors. But, for some ungodly reason, someone found it necessary to paint these floors with paint that looked to be the color of rusty pipe water. In some cases the paint would wear and instead of finding a way to restore the wood, Mom would go out and try to match the puke-colored paint. It was horrid.

But, these floors had been painted and re-painted; never once considering that perhaps they could have a layer of paint stripped off before applying another layer. Coat after coat of paint was applied until the floors were six-inches higher then when they were first installed. It's a wonder our heads weren't scraping the ceiling by the time we finally moved out.

Wherever there were floors that were not painted, there was linoleum. I'm not talking about high-grade, professionally installed linoleum. I'm talking "they had a sale down at the 10-Cent Store" piece-meal linoleum.

I can still see Dad laying that linoleum out and nailing it to the floor with those little black carpet tacks. This linoleum flooring became an indoor skating rink for us young'uns. We would love to take off running in our stocking feet and skate across the smooth linoleum surface. This was obviously more fun than the traditional method of walking from place to place.

However, this was only fun when we were actually planning to skate. It was not fun when we would enter the kitchen at 7 a.m., sleepy-eyed and about to have breakfast, only to have our feet ripped out from under us the moment we stepped onto the linoleum-covered floor.

Seeing the dilemma, Mom set out to correct the problem. Her solution was worse than the problem. She bought scatter rugs. Mom was sure these would provide sure footing and comfort to the feet.

There is a reason they call these "scatter rugs." The minute you step on them they scatter, taking your feet and legs with them. Mom had not provided a solution to the skating problem, she had provided a sled.

Many is the time that I walked into a room, stepped on a scatter rug and was instantly forced to become a contortionist, as I struggled to keep both legs pointed in the same direction.

I can't imagine why Mom would have these rugs. Most of the time they were lying wadded up in the floor. They had no backing. There was nothing that kept them attached to the floor. They were like big dust rags.

But, they were all over the house, especially in front of the sink. That certainly made sense. Where better to have a slippery pile of yarn than next to a porcelain sink? Imagine if you will, a 10-year-old boy running into the kitchen from outside, sweating and huffing, heading for the sink to get a cool drink of water.

At 10, I had no sense. I knew the scatter rug was there, but still I would make my approach to the sink much like a raging bull. Only after I had filled my glass would I suddenly be thrust into oblivion.

As kids we certainly needed no help in putting bruises and scrapes on our bodies, but whether we liked it or not, we got plenty of help.

The little brown house out back

It seems of all the things I have written about in my columns, the one topic that seems to draw the most response from people relates to the outhouse. Usually it is someone who is of the age to have had the experience of utilizing this wooden structure as a means of relief. But, I am happy that the outhouse is a part of my life experience. Most people my age and older did not have the unique opportunity to trudge outside in front of God and country and head for that humble little one-room relief station.

But, to me as a child, it was as necessary to my family as a dinner table or a bed. Ours was a single-seat model; Miss Addie Justice who lived next door had a two-seater. I have longed tried to understand the rationale behind a two-seater because to me, sharing the outhouse is far too personal an event to be shared with a companion. But, Miss Addie had two seats and even had curtains on a window. I am not sure, but it seems to me Miss Addie's outhouse also boasted of wallpaper, carpeting and a skylight. Well, maybe I am exaggerating a little on those points. Our outhouse had no window. It was my understanding that nothing took place inside the outhouse that required a view of the neighborhood.

We did however, have a knothole that had been shoved out of one of the wooden planks which allowed a stream of sunlight to break through on those warm summer days. Trust me, those of you who have not had the privilege of using an outhouse as your primary rest room facility cannot appreciate how wonderful it is to have some type of air vent, whether placed there on purpose or completely accidentally.

On summer days if you spent more than 15 minutes in the outhouse you either risked perishing from lack of oxygen or melting into a pile from the intense heat.

I could tell when company was coming. Mom was in the outhouse scrubbing the toilet seat linoleum. I suppose having clean, shimmering linoleum would help offset the fact that our visitors would have to hike outside and access a bathroom that was in reality, no more than a wooden bench with a hole cut in it.

We never considered it to be an embarrassment that my mother's aunt and uncle, who lived in the suburbs of Baltimore and had wonderfully operational indoor bathroom facilities, would be inconvenienced by having to use an outhouse.

Ours was a plain, ordinary outhouse, built by my grandfather. I do not think there were outhouse manufacturers per se, in those days. It was to each his own and property owners built their own outhouses. There were also few outhouses that had door knobs. There was usually a nail that stuck out to help you open and close the door, and a block of wood that turned on a nail to keep the door shut.

The outhouse has somehow come of age. I was inside a friend's house the other day and they had just redecorated their bathroom. Interestingly enough, the shower curtain and other amenities in the room were carrying a design of outhouses. These structures of the past have now become fodder for yard ornaments, household knick-knacks and a variety of other nostalgic items. They are now a fad fashion statement. However, when I was growing up they were far from fashion statements; they were crude, backyard buildings that sported more flies than two-day old road-kill.

There always seemed to be a hornet's nest hanging from the outhouse ceiling and a spider crawling somewhere. I had to spend my entire time inside the outhouse scanning floor to ceiling to avoid being attacked by some varmint. Then there was always the uncreative buffoon who found it hilarious to run a tree or bush branch up the back of the outhouse trap door while someone was using the facilities. They would always holler, "Snake!" as they rustled the branch back and forth, as if they were the first person to ever think of this prank.

Halloween always put our family on "outhouse watch," as every property in the town was faced with the prospect of having their outhouse tipped. Young heathens would patrol through the dimly lit backyards and like witless morons find outhouses to turn over. It presented a situation where you had to run to the outhouse on a Halloween night and get in and out as quickly as possible for fear the structure would be tipped over with you in it. I could think of no fate worse than having to crawl out from under an outhouse.

Another less than attractive feature that came as part and parcel of the whole outhouse theme was the use of the slop jar, which was as close as we could get to indoor facilities. Mom hated the task of having to empty the slop jar, which came with a couple of concerns. There was always the risk of dropping it halfway down the stairs and then the very embarrassing situations of being seen toting the slop jar out to be dumped.

I recall Mom's feeble attempts to get to the outhouse to empty the slop jar without someone seeing her. It was futile because we lived on Richardson Avenue, which was the main thoroughfare through the middle of Crisfield and a heavily populated residential area. It would have been easier for Mom to tote a sailboat through the backyard without being noticed than that slop jar.

No matter when she headed out the door somebody would be outside getting water from the cistern, or hanging clothes on the line, ready to start up a conversation, something that was uncomfortable to do with a slop jar in your hands.

I now own an outhouse and it sits directly behind my house. Each day as I come out of my back door I am able to pass by this wooden structure. It allows me to always remember where I came from; well, not really came from, but how I lived as a child.

The outhouse depicted on the cover of this book sits behind my home in Seaford. It was built for me as a gift by Ronnie Elliott, of Laurel, out of lumber taken from his girlfriend, the late Joyce Mears' father's home in Blades, Delaware.

We finally made it to the top

It was beautiful. It was the closest thing to Heaven that my young eyes had ever gazed upon. It was white, shiny and cool to the touch. At 10 years of age, I truly felt that my family had finally made it to the top. There I stood with my father, mother, two brothers and grandmother in total awe. It was like the President's Inauguration and Queen's Coronation all wrapped in to one. Shivers ran up and down my spine and my hair stood on end as Dad pulled the shiny silver lever and for the first time in the Windsor family's history a commode flushed.

To many I am sure it seems like a trivial event, but to me and my family having a toilet that sat inside the house was monumental. And as if that was not enough, sitting right next to it was an indoor wash tub. They were a matching set. The white porcelain was so shiny it hurt my eyes. For the first time in 10 years I would not be bathed inside the kitchen sink or out on the back porch in a big round bucket; both of which were done in full view of the neighbors and anybody who happened to be visiting my parents or grandmother.

Today, anything but an indoor toilet would be unthinkable. However, the idea that I would finally be able to sit on a toilet that had an actual seat was more than I could handle. If I am not mistaken, I think my family was so taken by the new indoor bathroom that instead of watching Ed Sullivan and Bonanza that first Sunday night, we all stood in a semi-circle and watched the toilet flush. I am not sure if we got used to it right away, or perhaps we kept a hornet's nest, a horde of flies and several spiders somewhere in the bathroom just to make us feel at home for those first few weeks. The bathtub was the equivalent of a swimming pool to us young'uns. When I was about three or four years old I suppose the outside #10 wash tub was pretty nice. However, the older I got the smaller the tub became. By the time I was 10 years old, it was all I could do to keep my legs and knees inside the tub. I had to become a contortionist to take a bath.

I think I said before that out of us three kids, I was always the last to get in the wash tub. Mom had to heat the bath water on the stove in the kitchen and walk it out pot by pot to fill the tub. There was no way she was going to even consider drawing more than one wash tub filled with water. She even threw our dirty clothes in with us and did the laundry while we took our bath. She was a pioneer in the water conservation effort.

So, one by one, we got into the water. When my youngest brother got in you could see the bottom of the tub. By the time my older brother had gotten in and out of the bath water it was a milky gray and there was enough sand on the bottom of the tub to raise crawdad. I recall soaking in the tub feeling like I was sitting on sandpaper.

The new indoor tub had its own running water. We could actually get fresh water for each bath. It was the first time I could remember being able to dunk my head underwater without having to recall with horror that my brothers had been in the tub just minutes earlier.

It seems funny now, but indoor plumbing was a major event in our household. It marked the first time that we had running hot water in the house and brought about the end of the traditional toting of the slop jar from upstairs and outside to the outhouse.

In my young mind I was sure there was no way life could get any better. I figured that if we could get an indoor commode and wash tub, the sky was the limit. Before you knew it I felt confident about dreaming that it would actually be possible for the Windsor family to enjoy such luxurious amenities as air conditioning and cable television. Yes, at 10 years of age I realized that we had truly arrived

You just can't trust a snake

There is an experience from my youth that never ceases to remind me of how silly I can be at times. Feel free to stop me if I've told this story before.

I was just about 16 years old and a diehard music fan. I could not go to sleep at night if I didn't have music playing. On this one particular night I had bought a new record and was excited to have these new tunes to listen to when I went to bed. Unfortunately, I learned that the needle on my record player was broken. This is after I had already stolen the needles from both my brother's and father's record players and worn those out. I was devastated.

However, I was fortunate to have a friend, Melissa Burnett, who lived down the road from me and owned a portable record player. It was about a mile or so down the road and I was very accustomed to walking to the Burnett's house to visit. So, on this evening I called Melissa and she graciously agreed to allow me to borrow her record player. Much to my great enthusiasm she was also willing to throw in a 45 RPM copy of "Long, Cool Woman in a Black Dress," by the Hollies. This was one of my favorite songs at the time. So, off to her house I walked. At about half way to her house I pass what appeared to be a massive pile of crawling black flesh. Upon closer observation, I realize that this was a couple of black snakes. It was late summer, mating season for the snakes. I didn't hang around long because I knew how aggressive these snakes could be during mating season. It was not beyond them to attack, so, on I moved.

Within about 20 minutes I was at Melissa's door. After a few minutes of small talk, she handed me the record player and off I went. By this time it had gotten dark, but happily, I headed back home, eager to listen to my new records. As I walked down the road, I suddenly felt a tugging at the back of my leg. I turned to see a long, black snake nipping at my leg. I was mortified.

I took off running at breakneck speed. However, to my shock the snake was still there. "My God, it has gotten its fangs hung up in the leg of my jeans," I thought to myself. I started running in a zigzag pattern, hoping to shake him loose. To no avail, still, he hung on. I then ran zigzagged and added some jumping up and down, shaking my legs in a "Mr. Bojangles" fashion. I ran frantically, believing this would certainly jar him loose. No such luck.

On I ran, "Run Forrest run." You can imagine the horror that I felt as I ran down the road with a full-length black snake attached to my trousers. Finally reaching my front yard, I stood in the middle of the yard, kicking and struggling.

As I looked down I could see by the glow of an outside florescent yard lamp the creature that had gotten a hold of me. This was the first light, other than moonlight, that I had been exposed to during my battle. As I looked down I saw it. It was a long, black, slender, electric cord connected to the record player. It must have fallen loose as I was leaving Melissa's house.

For the past 15 minutes I had been fighting off a wild electric cord. Man, I felt stupid. Oh well, who knows, it may well have been the mating season for electric cords!

My phone weighed 25 pounds

I was on the telephone the other day and it struck me just how much this communication device has changed since I was a little kid. I remember as a child the telephone was an ominous looking gadget, pitch black and weighing in excess of 25 pounds. There was no rotary dial or pushbutton keyboard on the device, only a round, white label situated at the center of the base which displayed our phone number, 39-W.

Interestingly enough, the phone lines in Crisfield, Md., in the early 1960s had not progressed to allow us individual lines. Our family shared our phone lines with three other families on Richardson Avenue. It just so happened that two of these families were comprised of the biggest gossip mongers in the community.

Each family was assigned a specific number of rings to identify when the phone was to be answered. For instance, I believe we had three rings which indicated the call was for us. Each time the phone rang you had to wait a few seconds before picking up to be sure of the number of rings so as not to pick up on someone else's call.

Many were the times you would go to pick up the phone just to hear the next door neighbor in the middle of a conversation. The polite thing to do was immediately hang up, not offer an apology, but hang up loudly enough for the neighbor to be aware you were no longer on the line. However, it was a tempting proposition to simply remain on the line and listen to the details of what I assure you was titillating news. I recall listening in as Miss Addie Justice gave Miss Dot Tawes her recipe for applesauce cake, and once when Elmer Lane was talking to Forbush's Hardware Store about paint for his garage.

You have to understand, I was very young and the biggest thrill for me and my brother was picking the phone up and hearing the operators say, "Number please." We would do this time after time and just laugh and laugh. The operator would grow weary of this and say with a very commanding voice, "You kids get off this line and stop playing with the phone." She would even call back and tell my mother what we were doing. We were simply uncivilized heathen young'uns.

My mother recalls the time she would be in the middle of a telephone conversation and hear the familiar click of someone picking the phone up. She would then not hear what should have been the loud click of this person hanging up. Not wanting to appear paranoid she would continue her conversation, leaving out the good stuff that she knew would fuel the ambitions of this unwanted third party.

I can recall that on one occasion my mother learned she was pregnant with my younger brother and shared information with her best friend, Pat Diggs, in a phone conversation. This was the first person who had been told outside of my father. About 15 minutes after finishing her phone call, Mom walked down to Miss Ruby Dize's store and was greeted by Miss Ruby, sitting in her chair. As Mom walked in Miss Ruby said, "So I hear your gonna have another baby." There is no doubt that the Crisfield Times had nothing on the Richardson Avenue party line crew.

I tried to imagine what it would be like today if we still had party lines and shared the airwaves with our neighbors. You would suddenly see the ratings drop on shows like Ricki Lake and Montel Williams. Everybody would be clustered around the telephone like hogs around a slop bucket, trying to find out all the latest gossip.

But, I guess that's something that has never changed throughout the ages. People's interest in knowing what we perceive to be the intimate details of other people's lives. I guess the gossip tabloids and shock gossip television talk shows can actually be traced back to the party lines of yesterday. To think, if we would have simply put a toll charge on the party lines we would be millionaires today.

Skidrow in the only photo he stood still long enough to have taken (1969, Crisfield).

Not much of a life for 'Skidrow'

Skidrow never had much of a life. When things start going badly for me I often think of that big lump of fur we called Skidrow. That dog was part Labrador, part locomotive train.

Once he was grown, my parents wasted no time getting Skidrow out of the house. We lived in as much of a residential neighborhood as you could get in Crisfield. There was no land-use plan in place in Somerset County, that's for sure. Houses were built on lots so small that our back porch steps were the front porch steps for the house behind us.

There was no way that Skidrow could be allowed to run free. His rambunctious behavior was certainly more than any of our neighbors could have stood. We tied Skidrow up to a chain we bought at the Silco store. Within ten minutes

23

he was loose. The links to the chain were stretched like pieces of rubber. I can still see Skidrow running like a banshee, dragging a broken length of chain behind him.

He moved with bullet speed. The first thing he would head for was laundry hanging on a clothes line. He would charge it like a ram in mating season. He would drag the laundry down, shake it and run with it clenched in his teeth.

Shooting Skidrow would have been the only way to appease the women who lived along Maple Avenue and Myrtle Street whose laundry lines looked like Dirty Harry's target range.

Once, after having withstood two full weeks of being locked up on his chain without a jail break, Skidrow broke loose. This was no small feat. By now Skidrow had broken away so many times that Dad had recruited the use of a steel cow chain. The chain had also been reinforced with a length of tow rope and a variety of discarded extension cords.

It was a beautiful Saturday morning and our next door neighbor, Mary Edith Mills, felt relieved that she had just brought her clean, sun-dried, breeze-fresh laundry in off the clothes line. On this particular day, Skidrow was once again on the lamb. Off my brothers and I went to hunt for the dog. We cornered him along Richardson Avenue, hut he knocked my little brother down and charged toward a field behind our house.

Skidrow ran through a parcel of marsh mud, stopping long enough to wallow in the nasty purplish marsh liquid. Now covered from head to paw in foul-smelling marsh mud, Skidrow continued leading us on a chase.

Because it was a warm spring day, Mary Edith had her doors open. Skidrow charged through her front door and into the hallway of her old, two-story house. In a room off to the right of the hallway Mary Edith stood, folding her beautiful white sheets, pillow cases and undergarments into neat stacks on the couch.

As if it was his duty, Skidrow barreled into the room, jumped on the couch and once again, wallowed, smearing fresh marsh mud on as many fresh, clean items as possible, Mary Edith screamed, throwing her hands and a brassiere she was holding into the air,

The brassiere came down, landing on Skidrow's head. He grabbed the strap and clenched it in his teeth. The dog then charged through the house and out the open back door. The parade that followed was made up of me directly behind Skidrow, followed by my older brother, my younger brother and last but not least, Mary Edith. She was screaming, ranting and carrying a broom in her hand. We were all chasing a big brown and white dog with a brassiere on his head.

A few months after this incident, my family moved in to our new home in Marion Station. The landscape was nothing but countryside. It was all open fields, something I am sure Skidrow could have only imagined in his dreams.

Only three days after moving into our new home, my brother and I were playing catch in the front yard. In his traditional playful manner, Skidrow chased a wildly thrown ball out into the road. In a split second our big bundle of energy laid silent and still, victim to a speeding motorist. Skidrow had finally met his match.

As we drove to the veterinarian's office in Pocomoke, Md., I sat in the backseat of the car holding Skidrow's head in my hands while his bulky body heaved as he struggled to catch his breath due to a punctured lung. This was the only time I could recall Skidrow ever staying in one place for any length of time. Almost as if by design, as we pulled up to the veterinarian's door and Dad turned off the car's motor, Skidrow took one last gasp of air and died.

I thought to myself, "Skidrow never had much of a life." But now as I recall how rambunctiously he lived his short, enthusiastic life, perhaps it was a little better than I thought.

Empty the trash, fill the ice trays?

There is a question that I have pondered for many years and have yet found an answer; perhaps someone wiser than I can solve this mystery.

How high above the kitchen garbage can does the trash need to be in order for it to be considered full?

I am amazed. I remember that when he lived at home, my son made an art out of balancing milk cartons, empty TV dinner boxes and soda cans on top of one another. This feat has only one goal in mind – not to be the one to take the trash out. It irritates me, but I guess the proverbial apple doesn't fall too far from the tree. I recall being the same way when I was a young boy.

I remember opening the basement door where Mom kept the trash can and blindly throwing trash at the can. Usually there would end up being a stack of trash at the bottom of the basement stairs the size of Mount Ararat. I could even look directly at the trash can, which would be filled above the rim, and still attempt to get another piece of trash inside. It would take me longer to balance the trash than it would have taken to empty the garbage can.

I think they should have "trash stacking" as an Olympic event. My son and I would bring home a guaranteed Gold Medal for the United States.

But it is not just trash that gets treated this way. I can remember Dad's pride and joy in the refrigerator was the ice water. He would fill old orange juice bottles with tap water and put them in the refrigerator. We would come inside from a hot summer's day, sweating like a CEO at a Senate hearing, and drink Dad's water.

The trick was to never drink the last drop of water. I would drink the water until it stood about one micro-meter above the bottom of the jug. I would then put it back into the refrigerator only to have Dad come in the kitchen 15 minutes later, raging, "Who was the last one to have the water?"

Of course we would all say in unison, "There was still some water in the jar when I put it back." When we talk about this scenario, we can't forget those all-important ice cube trays. You see, growing up in my house we had no air conditioning and the summers seemed hotter than Satan's sauna. So, when you were thirsty there was only one thing worse than finding the ice water jug empty. That would be finding the ice cube trays empty too. Long before the time when the refrigerator had its own ice maker, there were ice cube trays. You would pull the metal crank on the top of these contraptions to loosen the ice cubes. Nine times out of 10, someone would have filled the trays with too much water and the handle would be firmly frozen to the top of the tray.

I can't recall a time when I didn't scrape the skin off four of my knuckles trying to bust the ice loose. The trick here was to always leave at least one ice cube in the tray. That was assurance that I would not have to fill the ice tray.

However, when Dad went into the refrigerator and found his water jug empty, you could be sure his temper heightened when he discovered one lone ice cube in the tray. The thick, hot Crisfield tap water needed a minimum of six ice cubes to give any semblance of cool. I just can't figure out why it seemed such a major task to empty the trash or fill an ice cube tray or water jug. The same lazy people who do this are the very ones who leave a quarter-ounce of ice cream lodged in the corner of the box, a millimeter of milk in the bottom of the carton and 10 corn flakes in the bottom of the cereal box.

It is nothing less than torture to have become enticed with the thought of a dish of ice cream or a bowl of cereal, only to find the boxes are a mere facade for the emptiness inside. Oh well, I guess every family has at least one of these predators. You know who you are!

It's a generational plague. It's like heart disease; it's passed down through our genes. I know I will go home tonight and find a trash can over-flowing, toilet paper with one sheet left on the roll, a piece of soap the size of a quarter in the soap dish and enough underarm deodorant to do one armpit.

Oh well, it keeps me feeling needed.

What a real pain in the foot

I guess I don't have a huge pain threshold. I got up in the middle of the night last week and knocked a 16-ounce container of hair spray off the table. It was amazing. For the split second before the hair spray can reached my foot, I was able to recognize it as the 16-ounce container and breathed a sigh of relief because I knew it certainly could not be a major source of pain.

It was at the end of this split-second thought that the can hit my toe and immediately sent a shock wave of pain throughout my body. My toe began to thump with large throbs of pain and I quickly learned what they meant about concentrated weight. It felt like an anvil had fallen from the roof onto my toe. I guess it's my fault. I have the bad habit of waking in the middle of the night to get a drink of water, generally charging through the house like I have the radar senses of a bat. I don't think there is a piece of furniture I have ever missed.

There is something less than dignified about stubbing your toe on a chair leg. I have actually been creative in how I stub my feet. Sometimes I just lumber in and strike the old big toe on a nightstand, while other times I am able to run my entire foot under a low-lying couch, scraping the top of my arch all the way to my leg joint.

One of my favorites is staggering out into the darkness of the dining room and gracefully shoving the chair leg between my big toe and the toe next to it. I am still amazed by the fact that there is actually a scant milli-second that passes between the time you strike your toe on a piece of furniture and when you feel the pain. This means you actually have time to think about how bad this is going to hurt.

Another neat thing is that you actually see stars when you stub your toe. If it is dark when your toe hits the obstacle, there will be a quick flash of light inside your head. You can actually see it. I'm serious. Try it. Run into the living room with your eyes closed. Keep them closed, because it has to be dark. You will see the light I promise.

Of course, whenever I strike my body on a hard object in the presence of other people, I do not react the same way as when I am alone. For instance, the other day I was having my car worked on at the repair shop. I was in the car explaining to the mechanic what was wrong as he started looking under the hood. As I rambunctiously got out of the car I somehow struck the very top my head on the panel above the car door. This must be the most sensitive part of the body. It felt like someone had jabbed a sewing needle into the top my head.

I had to act like nothing had happened. I continue to talk to the mechanic while wincing and gnashing my teeth. I felt tears come to my eyes. I slyly brushed my hair with my hand, checking to see if there might not be blood dripping out of my wound. No blood. That's strange too, because I've actually found myself disappointed when finding there is no blood to go with the pain. I better stop. I'm starting to scare myself.

Preparation skills were lacking

When I was young my family never did vacations. There was no such thing. Vacations were something we saw on television. Chip and Ernie Douglas went on vacation with Uncle Charlie and Fred MacMurray and Granny and Uncle Jed vacationed in Hootersville.

For my brothers and me a vacation was a day's trip to Ocean City or a Saturday afternoon in Salisbury. I was always told that we didn't go on vacation because my father was a 'home body." The truth be known, my parents probably figured they could better keep their three nose-picking heathen young'uns at bay while at home than while on a road trip.

However, I was happy that before my father died we had opportunity to take family vacations. I was in my 40s, but they were family vacations nonetheless. We would all arrive at my Mom and Dad's home in Marion Station. The first thing we had to do was load up the van. One person's luggage was difficult to tell from another's because we all used the same brand grocery bags.

There is a system to this. For large items, like shirts, pants and shoes we would use the heavy paper grocery bags. For smaller items, like shampoo, razors and hairspray, we use the plastic grocery bags with the loop handles. If my mother has had a good week at yard sales, we might even encounter an authentic piece of luggage, handle actually included. I guess it has always been the nature of my family to be concerned only about having on hand those things it takes to get by on a day-to-day basis. Being prepared has always seemed like a luxury or, at limes, a waste of money.

For instance, somebody gets married, or somebody dies. To most families the first thing to do is to make note of the important date on the calendar so as not to miss the event. For my family the first thing to happen is a massive networking effort to pull together enough 'good clothes' to make the scene without looking like Homer and Jethro.

When I was a child, my mother would spend hours digging though me and my two brothers' clothes to see if between the three of us she could piece together one half-decent suit. My younger brother would end up with my shirt, my older brother's pants and my father's shoes. He looked like a police composite sketch.

Because of my size I would almost always have my father's pants and shirt, with a tie that he probably wore when he met my mother. The tie was always one of those massively wide ones with loud pastel flower designs. Try as my mother would, it was difficult for me to attend a formal event without looking like Bozo the Clown.

Then there was poor Dad. He was the only one who had anything remotely resembling dress clothes. So, we rummaged through his wardrobe like Juan Valdez picking coffee beans. We always wore tennis shoes, or those clodhopper-looking, pale orange work boots. So, we had to borrow Dad's black dress shoes whenever we went to church or other formal affairs. It meant nothing that they didn't fit. Often was the time Morn would stuff toilet paper in the toes of the shoes to keep them from flopping on and off my feet as I walked.

I guess it was all my parents could do to pull enough money together to keep clothes on our backs for everyday use, let alone waste money on clothes that would only get worn if someone died. So, it is easy to understand that when we headed out for vacation, we had not done a great deal of preparation. As long as the van moved and all four tires were where they belonged, off we would go. It didn't take much to make our vacation a successful affair. If we could get there without losing one of the young'uns and there was a restaurant where we could stuff our faces, we were happy. It's good to be country at heart.

My family vacations remind me of something Jeff Foxworthy once said about his family vacations: "When you get all my family together for a vacation, you know there must be an empty Wal-Mart somewhere.' Oh well, when you live simple, it's easier to be satisfied.

It was an electrifying experience

I have often written in my columns about the voracious appetites that existed among me and my brothers. It seems eating was to us like breathing is to most people. As a young boy growing up in Somerset County, I would find myself at my grandparent's house every Sunday, where the entire Windsor family gathered to graze like so many oxen in a field.

It was a family ritual that started at about noon and lasted until sometimes as late as 10 or 11 o'clock at night. My grandmother could be found trudging around the small kitchen pulling the lids off of what now seem like several dozen pots and pans. There would be a huge, oval shaped pot filled with greasy dumplings and potatoes boiling in a neighboring pot. There was chicken frying and biscuits baking, all taking place on top of, and inside of, a black cast iron stove that was fueled by wood.

As the Windsor daughter in-laws arrived, they would begin to help my grandmother and the kitchen soon looked like a County Fair Bake-Off. Young'uns were not allowed in the house while dinner was cooking. Actually we were barely allowed in the house while dinner was being served.

It was traditional for the Windsor grownups to eat before any of us young'uns even saw a plate. So, you can imagine the slim pickings that were available once we charged to the dinner table. I think we were lucky to wind up with chicken neck bones and feet. But, that was the way it was. In my youth it was not only a point that young'uns were "seen and not heard," but if possible, we were not even seen.

So, we would go outside and play while food cooked and the grown-ups chatted inside my grandparent's house. Sounds almost like a Norman Rockwell painting, huh? Well, not necessarily. You see, there is nothing quite like the concept of having upwards of 20 or more heathen young'uns running around in the farm yard and neighboring fields like a bunch of epileptic goats. What piece of meanness one could not think of; there was a dozen more to consider it.

Horses and cows prodded with corn stalks, chickens and ducks dodging rocks and dirt clods, there was no end to the ornery antics of me and my brothers and cousins. There were plenty of ditches that we could push one another into, and a bountiful supply of steaming cow and horse manure piles that were perfect places to "accidentally" trip an unsuspecting victim.

I suppose I was as impish as any of my other young Windsor counterparts and certainly spent enough of my time trying to grab the fish out of my grandfather's backyard concrete fish pond. So, I guess if any of us became victims of our own hellish behavior, there was no one to blame but ourselves.

Such was the case when at the age of about five, while taunting my grandfather's pony, "Papoose," from the other side of the fence; I leaned too close to the electrically charged wire. I am not sure if you know what happens when you make contact with an electric farm fence, but I will describe the reaction. It is as if a great big hand suddenly out of nowhere grabs you extraordinarily abruptly and holds you in place while a great big fist pounds you all over your body. It is a constant beating that lasts as long as you are attached to the fence wire. So, I was literally hanging upside down with the fence wire under my stomach, beating me like 25 pounds of bread dough. Luckily my cousin, Kerry, saw my dilemma and ran for help. Hanging over the fence I remember looking between my dangling feet and watching as grownups poured out the front door of the house like drug dealers at a SWAT raid.

The power was cut off and my father pulled me off the wire. I think for the next couple of days I staggered instead of walked and it was a long time before my arms stopped flinching. It was a very horrific experience.

Although it was apparently not too horrific, because the Windsor's returned to their meal and left me outside to bide my time until I joined the other young'uns for dinner. Oh well, so much for parental pity.

Not just another fish story

It is nice to hear from people who have read my columns and take the time to say "hello" in the store. There are usually two questions that I can expect to hear from most people when they speak to me. One is to ask whether my columns are reflective of the truth, or do I make things up as I go along. The other questions are usually asked about whether I really got beat by my parents as often as I say in my columns.

Well, let me clear the air. Number one, yes everything is true that I write in my columns. Also, yes I did get beat as many times I have chronicled in my writings. But, I must also say that you have to put this all into proper perspective. First of all, I write weekly about events that took place over about 18 years of my life. So, if it is seems that I spent every day in some kind of trouble that may be a slight exaggeration. But, once again for the record, I will state that I did not get beat more often than I got in trouble.

It was a one-to-one ratio. I only got beat when I deserved it. Thus, the reason why it appears I was abused. On the other hand, there were many times when I did something I shouldn't have and never got caught. These instances were few and far between, but still did occur. It was harder for me because my father was a policeman and he had a built in instinct for detecting wrongdoing.

Although it wasn't really all that hard because with three heathen boy young'uns there was bound to be trouble at some point each and every day. I think we worked in shifts. I must have had the weekend shift because it seems that was when I got in the most trouble.

I would even get in trouble when I didn't mean to. Like the day I backed into my father's prized stack of fish aquariums. He had a metal shelf that held two fish aquariums; one on top of the other. I can still recall the soft, gurgling sound that the water filter pump made as it cleaned the water. I would spend hours staring into the fake ocean bottom, watching the array of brightly colored fish swimming around the toys that Dad kept on the bottom. There was a toy treasure chest with a lid that would open and close and a miniature diver who would bob up and down, powered by the air filter pump.

I would become enamored by the tropical fish that were like a circus sideshow. There was a small catfish with giant whiskers, the black fish with a head like a hammer and the fish that stuck to the side of the tank, sucking all the crap off the sides and bottom of the fish tank.

Then it happened. I was too busy throwing a couch pillow at my brother to notice that I was too close to the aquariums. All at once my brother chucked the pillow. I lunged back to miss being hit and drove my heel into the front of the aquarium glass. It was like someone had flushed the Inner Harbor aquarium into our living room. Fish were flying and flopping around like, well, like fish out of water. Tiny black and orange pebbles came rushing out into the floor. I was mortified. Not only was it Dad's prized fish aquarium, but it was also Mom's living room floor.

I think this was the one time in my young life that I actually screamed. I mean I screamed without getting beat. Mom came running with a mop and bucket, grabbing fish off of the floor like a tomcat in a seafood shack. She was too busy trying to stop the oncoming catastrophe to deal with me. Meanwhile I was dancing around the floor like I was on fire.

I knew I had hit the mother lode of trouble. I was in the big time now. I would be lucky if I was able to walk to school the next morning. Luckily Mom was too tired to do more than scream at me for about an hour and a half. But sometimes I would rather have been plowed in the head with a right hook from Joe Frazier than deal with that nerve-racking punishment.

When Dad came home that night it was after midnight and I was fast asleep. I went to bed imagining that he would come home and yank me out of a sound sleep and beat me unconscious. However, Dad never addressed me about that incident. He didn't replace the aquarium, but put the fish that survived into the other fish tank.

Eventually, the fish in that tank died and fish aquariums went the way of Dad's toy railroad trains, never to be heard from again. I almost believe that the sight of me cringing and running around the living room like I was being chased by a two-headed bear was something that Mom relayed to Dad. Whatever the reason, I don't care. It was one of those one in a million times that dad kept his belt on until he took his pants off to go to bed and that's all I care to know.

Mosquito spray and ice cream

I remember that while growing up in Crisfield, Md., summer time brought more than just the heat for us to battle. There were mosquitoes and horse flies to contend with. I can recall getting bit by mosquitoes to the point I would look like a huge welt with eyes. It was somewhat of a ritual. I would spend the day getting eaten up by mosquitoes and horse flies and then spend the night digging the welts till they bled.

I suppose I did little to avoid the attacks. I never wore a shirt and was constantly clothed in nothing but a pair of shorts. So, there was plenty of flesh for the mosquitoes and flies to feast on. I never wore shoes, although my feet would get so dirty it would appear that I was wearing a pair of boots.

Looking back I have to imagine that we were a ghastly sight in the neighborhood. I would play in the hot sun, sweat rolling and dirt caked on like another layer of skin. I had sweat beads running around my neck like a cheap necklace. You could have planted corn in the dirt I accumulated in my hair.

I know it must have gotten awful hot because I can recall sitting on the porch with my mother and grandmother and it was almost like Jesus' second coming when a breeze would blow. As the slight air of the breeze hit our face, Mom and my grandmother, almost in unison, would utter "oohs" and "aahhs" and exclaim how wonderful the breeze felt. I guess it says something for the amount of excitement we experienced in Crisfield when sitting on the porch judging breeze levels was the activity of the day.

Of course when the Ice Cream Man's musical tune could be heard from down the street, we all got excited. Mom would give me and my older brother some money and everybody would put in their orders. My grandmother would always get a Fudgesicle™ and Mom would want a Nutty Buddy™ ice cream cone or a Creamsicle.™

Of course my brother and I were given no choice. It was whatever cost a nickel. Usually we would end up with one of those frozen ice Popsicles.™

I remember standing in line at the side of the ice cream truck like we were picking up government milk and cheese. We would get the order and instead of rushing right back home with the ice cream, I would have to open my ice cream and start eating it while balancing the other treats as I walked down the street. By the time I got back to my front porch there was Popsicle juice running down my face and arms. Mom and Grandmom's ice cream was so soft they couldn't get the wrapper off without losing half of the ice cream.

Looking down the road we could see off in the distance the mosquito sprayer coming. This was the most unbelievable thing as I look back. This is guaranteed to be a thing of the past given today's concerns about pollutants in the air and groundwater runoff.

Here was a pickup truck with a huge machine on the back. The truck would come down the road and release a billowing, thick, white cloud of insecticide which would cover the area like a blanket of smog.

We would have to wheel my grandmother into the house and Mom would quickly shut the windows to escape the fog. You would think that we as young'uns would be ordered into the house and made to cover our faces with a gas mask, but, that was not the case.

My brother and I would hide behind a bush and wait for the "mosquito truck." When the truck would ride past and open the tank releasing the huge cloud, we would run out behind the truck and dance through the cloud like drunken apes. We were literally engulfed in poisonous toxins, running along like we were dancing in a spring rain. I have to wonder how either of us grew past the age of 10 without developing a second head.

Oh well, I guess when it comes to entertaining yourself at a young age, you just have to make the best with what you have to work with.

Winter: Snow and Dad's socks

I love the fall. It is my favorite time of the year. I am especially fond of early fall when the temperatures are not too cool and not too warm. The leaves are changing and beginning their descent to the ground. But, as I ponder this I also cannot help but realize that make no mistake, winter is coming. It brings to mind the winters of my youth. I am sure I have broached this before, but it makes me feel so warm and fuzzy inside to talk about it.

It would get so cold the snot would freeze on my upper lip. It was amazing that the minute I sensed it was getting cold; my nose would start to run. At age 6, most kids could simply blow their nose and the worst was over. However, for me it was more like draining sap from a maple tree. The more I rubbed the more of it that streamed out. But, that was a minor challenge in my wintertime trials.

Most people associate the thoughts of a white winter snow with the word "beautiful." I have to agree that seeing the sun glistening off a new fallen snow does create somewhat of a soothing image. As a child I could not wait to see the snowflakes start to fall. This represented many potential opportunities. If it were after the first snowfall of the year, Mom would make snow cream (snow with vanilla extract, cream and sugar). Snow would also bring about the possibility of school being closed. The possibilities were endless.

Perhaps the single most exciting outcome of a good winter's snow was found lying about 200 yards behind my house. In the spring and summer, it was adorned with grass, weeds and branches. But, when winter rolled around the huge pile of plowed trees had the definite features of a mountain.

When I was very young there was about an acre of field behind my house that we called "The Jungle." Actually as I recall it was somewhat of an eerie phenomena. The cover was not really trees, but more like tall, thick weeds. To a three-foot young boy they were more like redwoods. That field still remains a consistent image in my mind. And just like when I was a boy, that image conjures up all kinds of intense, frightening and mysterious thoughts. I guess it was because the growth was so thick that we could only imagine the horrid creatures that preyed around inside, especially in the darkness of night.

Then one day, with no advance notice, the bulldozers moved in and tore every tree and weed down and pushed it into a huge pile. Suddenly the unknown was no more than an empty field. The only remnant of that spooky playground of the demons was that big pile of various stages of brush.

In the summer it was our army fortress, but in the winter it became a ski lodge. I remember the winter of 1964. I was seven years old and we had a major blizzard. The snow was up past my thighs and drifts had blown against the house there no less than window height. It was not a playful desire, but more of a mission, that we conquer that big mountain which lie behind my house.

Now bear in mind, when I was a child our hands were covered with brown cotton gloves. Oftentimes I would lose my gloves by the time the snow came. It really didn't matter because those cotton gloves were as effective in the snow as a pair of boxing gloves. The first touch of snow rendered them soaking wet and could be likened to having your fingers shoved into a bucket of ice. One thing was for sure, if you lost your gloves, or they became wet, there were no thoughts of running to the closet or the store for another pair.

When you had no gloves it was time to wear a pair of Dad's winter socks. Boy, this was a treat. They did not fit like a glove or a pair of mittens. They fit like a sock.

But gloves were not the only things we came up short on. Winter boots were about as plentiful as 100-dollar bills.

So, when it came time to sled down the big mountain, would you think we would actually have a genuine sled? Not hardly. Once again, we improvised. The closest thing to a sled that we could find was a trashcan lid. Little did I know that I was about to embark on the single most treacherous ride of my young life.

I remember well trudging up the hillside carrying the silver trashcan lid. I realized as I made it to the top that even though the hill's terrain was littered with tree stumps and roots, I had to go. I carefully set the trashcan lid down on the hilltop. While my friend Carey held the lid, I climbed aboard. He gave me a shove and I flew off the lid and rolled down the hill like so many pounds of potatoes. There is no doubt to this day, that I struck every branch and stump on my way down. When I reached the bottom of the hill, I looked back up the hill to see one of Dad's winter socks hanging off a tree branch and Carey holding the trashcan lid.

It was a horrendous episode. The first thing I did was to pick myself up off the ground, stagger to my feet and head back up the hill for another roll. I could only wish that I had that level of tenacity today. It must not have been too bad, because I don't recall ever asking for a sled for Christmas. Oh well, youth is wasted on the young.

Pain was a constant companion

It seemed like a good idea at the time. After all, I had watched many characters on Saturday morning cartoons jump from buildings and float safely down to the ground holding an umbrella. So, I stood valiantly on top of Miss Townsend's outhouse, umbrella in hand. Though it seemed miles to the ground, I was confident that my umbrella would provide the parachute safety that would make my dissent a successful one.

As my brother Tommy watched from below, I leaped from the roof of the outhouse. I was shocked to learn, quite quickly I might add, that the slow, floating trip down to the ground turned into a split second of time followed by misery.

I fell to the ground like a 100-pound bag of stones. One moment I was looking out over the field behind my house; the next second I was part of the field behind my house. The first sensation I can remember feeling once my feet left the outhouse roof, was the sudden uptake created by the ground. Immediately the breath was knocked out of me and I frantically flayed around on the ground like a hypochondriac at a medical convention.

Once I was able to gasp for a few breaths of air, I started checking to see if I still had two arms, two legs and a head. It was terrible. Of course it provided great amusement for my brother who by now was dancing around like a cat in a fish house.

But, my young life was wracked with this type of pain. I experienced more tragedy than a peg-legged man in a minefield. My whole existence was wrought with misery. In the summer I would run around barefoot only to jam a rusty nail so far into my foot that dad would have to pull it out with a pair of pliers.

One day I was out back with my brothers while my mother sprayed us with a garden hose. This was as close as we got to a swimming pool; unless you count the big wash bucket we took baths in on the porch. Mom was spraying us with water and we were running around like apes on crack. All of a sudden I stepped on a broken Pepsi™ bottle and sliced my foot from ankle to big toe.

Neither the nail impaled foot, nor the foot that suffered severe mauling were serious enough to go to the hospital. Mom soaked them in warm salt water and stuck a Band-Aid™ over the wounds. That was it. I guess if we had gone to the hospital every time we had an accident we would have had a wing at McCready Memorial Hospital with our names on it. In my young life I had slammed my fingers in doors of every description from car doors to garage doors. I had struck my head on everything from windowsills to baseball bats. I had been struck in the head with flying dirt clods, rocks and clamshells. I had been thrown from a bicycle and a horse more times than an extra on Gunsmoke.

I have always felt growing up was more of a challenge for my brothers and I than most other kids. This was not because we were any more fragile than other kids; but more because we tempted fate at a higher rate than most normal people.

I mean the fact that we lived on Richardson Avenue, the busiest roadway in the town never left us cause to be careful. I liken us to geese. If you have ever watched geese cross a road you will notice they do it in an almost arrogant manner, oblivious to anything but their intended goal at the other side of the road.

If we were ever given a nickel it was somewhat comparative to being given the keys to a new Ford Explorer. I can recall taking off from the living room of my house and never stopping until I was standing in Archie Tyler's store. I would be darting through oncoming traffic like a thief in an episode of "Law and Order." I had no fear.

Oh well, I guess I managed to survive it. My mom always said I never got hurt too bad because I was so mean. Maybe she had a point.

Dad don't play

There were several things that instilled total respect and the "fear of God" in me as I was growing up. These included, but were not limited to, Dad's belt, Dad's hand and Dad's foot. I loved Dad, there is no doubt, but I think I respected him even more.

It was not only that he sported a green and black Maryland State Trooper's uniform most every day, or that his war medals could be found and marveled at as they lay tucked neatly away in an upstairs trunk. It was Dad's simple, but commanding presence. It was also that he had as much tolerance for our heathen behavior as he had patience. It never failed that when I would finally get it through my thick head that I had to find some possible way to keep from upsetting Dad, one of my brothers would do something to enrage him and put him in a bad mood. When Dad was in these types of moods he carried a very intimidating facial expression. It was something like a cross between Satan and a rabid Pit Bull.

Make no mistake about it; to me Dad was one of the greatest men to ever live. He was a hard worker who was totally committed to family. But, he was also dedicated to making sure his young'uns grew up with a healthy dose of respect; even if it killed them.

That is nearly why on several occasions I thought I was about to meet Jesus. The one such incident that stands out the most clearly in my mind is the night I called Dad a "pig." Now, bear in mind, this was not "pig" in the sense of the animal. It was during the early 1970s and there were people who referred to police officers as "pigs" in a very derogatory manner.

Dad had a thing about curfews. As a teen he set my curfew at 11:30 p.m. on the weekends. I used to argue that things didn't start getting fun until around midnight. He always told me that anything that was going on after 11:30 p.m. was something I did not need to be a part of. I would break curfew and Dad would ground me for a week. So, throughout my teen years I went out every other week.

I remember like it was yesterday one night that I came home well after curfew and as I walked in the kitchen I could see the glow of Dad's cigarette from the living room. I knew then there was going to be trouble. Sometimes Dad would be sleeping when I came in late and he would accost me the next morning to remind me that I had not gotten away with breaking curfew.

If Dad was up waiting when you got home late it meant only one thing; you better start thinking quick or prepare to stand at the throne of God. I guess as Dad came through the dining room and bolted toward the kitchen, I realized I had nothing to lose, so I developed an attitude. That was my first mistake, but there were several others that quickly followed in fast succession. Dad began to tell me that he was tired of me disregarding his rules and coming home whenever I pleased. He then immediately starting commenting about the "trouble makers" I was hanging out with at night. I am sure these other individuals were probably being tongue lashed by their parents for hanging out with me as well.

Dad then informed me that I would not be going out for the next two weeks. It was then that I made a fatal mistake. It was almost the last mistake I ever made in this life. I told

Dad that I was sorry that I could not be as perfect as him and the other "pigs" that he worked with.

It was as if God struck thunder down at that very precise moment. Dad grabbed me and hung on to me like a bull dog on a pork chop. He rolled me through the kitchen and out into the dining room like he was being paid for it. I remember him drop kicking me back into the kitchen and then coming at me with his black leather belt. That alone was a surprise attack because at the time Dad was wearing nothing but his boxer shorts.

I had on thick, heavy blue jeans, so Dad was clearly at an advantage. Long story short, by the time Dad got done beating me I was looking around to see who all had joined in on the fray. He hit me so fast, hard and furiously that I believe I was begging for "everybody" to please stop.

I was happy to inform Dad that from that moment on, as far as I was concerned, "pig" stood for "Pride, Integrity and Guts." It was also the last time I ever gave even a passing thought up standing up to my Dad.

First day of the rest of your life

I remember well when I was about 16 years old, my high school history teacher, Mr. Ed Crockett, told my class and I that we were "eating our white bread" at that stage in our lives. I have no idea what he meant by this phrase; except that he must have been referring to how easy life was for us at that time.

No bills, no worries about where the next meal would come from and so on and so forth. Nope, I certainly had no idea just how "good" I had it with two parents and a grandmother at home who made sure I did not have to consider issues related to survival. I know they must have struggled at times, but they never made us young'uns aware of it.

I have recognized over the past several years just how valuable that type of childhood stability was in terms of helping to provide support. The problem is I did not use that support to my advantage. The smart thing would have been for me to begin planning a path forward when I was about 16, while still enjoying the comforts of home, to ready myself for a world in which I was the primary caretaker. Instead I was hell bent for leather to make every moment from my teen years on as fun as possible.

Having the benefit of hindsight, I now have the one thing that everyone seems to acquire at one time or another, but very few can appreciate experiencing, and that is regrets. I suppose the one true benefit to regrets and mistakes are to have lessons learned, however, at some point I fear that some of life's mistakes are terminal.

For that reason, I would encourage young people, especially those between the ages of 16 and 18, to really take stock in their life and seek to answer the question, "Where would I like to be in 10 years"? If you are as fortunate as I was at that age, to have parents or guardians who are keeping the survival burden off of your shoulders for the time being, take advantage of it and grasp as much education and work experience as possible while this is still the case.

Recognize what it is you enjoy doing the most and try to make that the first goal in terms of a work career. I truly feel that doing something you really enjoy as a career is an added bonus to a paycheck. It is certainly much more enjoyable than spending your life doing whatever you have to do in order to keep the wolves away from the door.

I know that traditionally I use my column to write some humorous, light-hearted tale from my childhood. I love that I have this opportunity and so greatly appreciate those people who stop me on the street to say they read and enjoy the column. Words cannot express my heartfelt appreciation for these humbling experiences.

However, not every experience in life is particularly humorous. The only thing worse than those negative experiences that occur to all of us and are totally out of our control, are those in which we could have actually changed the tide and avoided the pain and disappointment, had we been better prepared.

I know that for the most part, my words will fall on deaf ears. However, I grow weary from experiencing the tribulations that past mistakes have created for me. For that reason, I would like for just one young person to truly recognize that "today is the first day of the rest of your life." Please know that what you accomplish today can very well impact your position in life 20, even 30 years from now. As much as it pains some of you, education and school are the first steps to life-success. How much success depends on how tightly you embrace this gift. My advice would be to get greedy and suck every ounce of learning you can from your teachers and other mentors. Remember, after high school the only free education comes by way of experience. Believe me, the "School of Hard Knocks" can be a very tough course to take.

Bottom-line, if you have anyone willing to offer you educational opportunities or work experiences, grab it like a bundle of money. I assure you, that in the scheme of life, it is worth so much more.

No fire prevention poster child

Living in the city limits of Seaford, Delaware, I am privy to the sound of the occasional siren signaling that there is an emergency of some kind in the area. This alarm unfortunately can be heard at all hours of the day and night. The tragic part of this is not the sound itself, but what that sound means. It means someone somewhere is most likely in a serious, dangerous situation. It also means that people in our community, like those all around us, are leaving the comfort of their homes to answer the call.

As I sometimes sit and consider the seriousness of the sacrifices made by the fire department personnel I recall just how careless I was as a young boy with fire and how I sometimes used it as a source of entertainment.

Growing up in Crisfield, Md., I was far from a fire prevention poster child. Unfortunately, like a lot of young people, I was very curious about fire. I can remember Dad always having an old 55-gallon drum for burning trash. It was orange from rust, with a charcoal rim from the flames that were often leaping from the top. Mom and Dad always warned my brothers and me to not play around the fire. They might have well told us that the smoke was layered with five-dollar bills. The second Dad went in the house we were frolicking around the burning trash drum like buzzards around a deer carcass.

At first we would find sticks and prod at the burning rubbish, sending glowing ashes into the night sky. Little by little, we would get braver and start to send quickly constructed paper airplanes into the top of the 55-gallon drum. I recall the time my brother, Tommy, and I were playing around the fire drum and a piece of burning paper leaped out of the drum and flew six-feet away from the can.

It set the grass on fire and I immediately ran to try and stop the flames. Of course I had about as much knowledge about how to treat a brush fire as I did about building a nuclear reactor. I ran and found an old plastic swimming pool and headed for the flames. By this time the flames had formed a half circle and were heading for the next door neighbor's house. I took the plastic pool and started beating at the flames to try and put them out. Of course the key word here is beating. The more I beat, the more wind was created. Before I knew it the flames covered an area three times the size it had been just seconds earlier. I became frantic.

I hollered for Tommy to get some water. He ran to the outside spigot and began bringing water and we started a fire brigade. Some brigade. It was me and my brother and a 12-ounce orange juice can. It took a quarter of a second to dump the water on the galloping flames and a minute and a half to go and get some more water. It was like the fire alarm rang and Laurel and Hardy responded.

I started envisioning the fire engines pulling up with hoses and ladders. Only in my vision fire engine pulled up and Dad beat me with the hoses and ladders. I was scared to death. All of a sudden, from out of nowhere came a blast of water. Dirt, mud and smoke flew. I turned and my father was using a garden hose to drown the flames. His only words were "Get up to the house…. NOW!"

I recognized the tone of my father's voice. He was usually holding a belt when he spoke like that and I know what he did with the belt once the words had been spoken. Here he was holding a 15-foot, triple reinforced, rubber garden hose.

There was no way I was going to stay around and wait for what was coming next.

The amazing thing is, Dad came back into the house a few minutes later, walked up to me and my brother and said, "You know what I told you about playing around the fire." He then went into the living room and read his paper.

Now, there would be some who might question this parental reaction. It doesn't seem too harsh for a couple of heathens who tried to burn down Richardson Avenue. But, what you might not realize is that Dad was very smart. Dad knew that my brother and I were not convinced of what our fate might be.

We didn't know whether Dad simply felt we were already scared enough to have learned our lesson, or whether on some dark night, while lying in the comfort of our bed, Dad's belt might strike like a match on dry grass. So, for the next few weeks, my brother and I were constantly looking over our shoulder. Because with Dad, when you least expected it... expect it.

Were we heating all outdoors?

As I passed through the small hallway that connected the kitchen and the living room, it struck me. Slicing into my soul like a carving knife was the harsh reality that I had somehow performed the unthinkable winter crime – I forgot to shut the backdoor. To make matters worse my father was home.

Even though we lived in a house that had more cracks and gaping holes than the surface of the moon, to my father leaving a door open was comparable to chucking a bucketful of money out the attic window.

I spun around and tried to make my way back to the kitchen door before Dad became aware of my terrible mistake and took to beating me like a five dollar drum. Just as I approached the door I heard those all too familiar words, "You better damn site shut that door. We're not heating all outdoors!"

Throughout my childhood I pondered with great meditation the concept of "heating all outdoors." Dad said it so many times that I came to believe it was something that could actually be done. However, it only took a few weeks of being on my own with my own home, to realize that heating a house with an open door was in reality, most like chucking a bucketful of money out the attic window.

Today I subscribe to a weather service on my computer which tells me the current outdoor temperatures as well as the forecasted temperatures for the day and week. This way I am able to determine how to dress before heading out to meet my day.

When I think back on my childhood home I am reminded that there was no need for such technology; we were constantly aware of the weather and temperature conditions. I could sit in the living room and tell how fast and in what direction the wind was blowing by comparing the shaking and rattling of the windows with the direction the curtains were blowing.

When we awoke in the morning my brother and I could tell how much it had snowed by the amount of snow that was piled up under the window inside our bedroom. It would get so cold that my grandmother's false teeth would freeze in their soaking bowl. Bottom line, winter was cold at our house.

Throughout the year, Dad had what we came to call seasonal jobs. These were certain tasks that had to be done at different times during the year and came to be a household tradition. For instance, Dad's summer job was not just cutting the grass and trimming the hedges like most traditions that continue today. He also had the esteemed responsibility of digging a big hole in the backyard and burying the residual materials that were piled up inside the outhouse. Talk about a crappy job!

So, in the winter time, in addition to shoveling snow and thawing frozen water pipes, Dad performed the annual duty of closing off the cracks around windows and doors. The winterization of our home consisted of Dad stapling sheets of heavy plastic across the windows. You could tell this was an annual chore because the staples from the previous years would still be jutting out from the window frames and sills. Once the plastic was up, looking out the window was limited and if you were visiting our home for the first time, could scare you into thinking you had cataracts.

Dad would then go to work to assure that there was no heat escaping outside the numerous and huge cracks around our heavy front door. To accomplish this he would round up as many newspapers and comic books as were available around the house. He would then stuff the newspapers and comic books into the cracks around the door. You can imagine what this looked like when he was finished. It looked like a living room door with comic books and newspapers sticking out from all sides.

It was not a pretty site and made the front door inaccessible. However, though the plastic on the windows and comic books and newspapers around the door left a lot to be desired in terms of household beauty, it did the job. The heat stayed inside and so did Dad's money!

Flip-flops and sweat beads

The past few weeks have had days where it seemed the sun was about to make landfall in my back yard. When you are in the midst of a hazy, hot and humid summer day, your first thought is that this has got to be the hottest it has ever been. But, when I am sitting in my air conditioned living room, I realize that there were hotter days – to me these were the summers of my youth.

The dirty sweat beads around my neck were thick enough to hang ornaments on and my feet were so dirty that it looked like I was wearing socks. Such was my normal appearance as a child on any given day beyond the last day of school.

Once the summer set in, you would find me and my brothers wearing stretch-waist shorts and little else. Mom and Dad made sure we sported crew cut haircuts so it lessened the chance of our getting cootie bugs. I think the single most embarrassing points in my mother's life were taking us young'uns to get haircuts at Ira Lowe's Barber Shop on 4th Street.

We would sit up in the big cushioned barber chair and as Ira Lowe began trimming off the already scalp-close hair, Mom would be the first one to spy the beads of dirt and sweat that formed around our necks. It looked more like we were wearing a string of charcoal. As he brushed our hair, enough sand and dirt fell out to plant a row of corn.

Mom would sit there humiliated that anyone would see how nasty her young'uns were. But, there was little that could be done about it. When we played outside we were not happy unless we had rolled around on the ground like we were on fire. What dirt we didn't roll around in, we scooped up and chucked at one another.

But, Ira Lowe never commented on how dirty out heads were, he just shaved them and gave us a dime for our trouble. It was like we were selling our hair. I never understood why this man would give us a dime when we got our haircut; especially when the haircut at the time probably only cost about 50 cents.

I guess as children we did not comprehend what it meant to maintain some sense of personal hygiene. I suppose getting dirty is pretty normal for most young people, but for us it was an understatement. We were not satisfied to simply be dirty, by day's end we looked more like street urchins from the set of Oliver Twist than normal children. You know you are dirty when your mother has to actually hose you down outside before she will let you in come in the house to get cleaned up.

We never wore shoes in the summertime and more often than not, the shorts we were wearing during the summer were previously the long pants we wore during the fall and winter. There was no new wardrobe come summertime. I think if the shorts were too small we would just run around in our underwear.

For footwear we were each assigned a pair of rubber flip-flops. Notice I did not refer to this foot garment as sandals. These were flip-flops, so called because of the flip-flop action and noise that came as you walked down the street. I think Mom bought them at Grants or Silco and they were made so cheap that the only way she really could have gotten her money's worth would be to have had them come with feet.

Actually I think Mom liked them not only because they were a cheap, almost dispensable form of summer footwear, but also because they were so handy for whacking us with when she did not have a flyswatter or yardstick handy.

All in all, summertime still sticks out in my mind as a time of non-stop action and outdoor fun that along with keeping us dirty, kept us entertained. There were no video games, Internet, or 100-channel televisions to keep us in the house. Come to think of it, maybe it would not be a bad idea to convince some of our young people today to put down the video games and computer controls and go outside and try on a dirty sweat bead necklace.

Dad, always up to the challenge

I really did have a deep respect for my elderly school teachers, perhaps because I was raised with a certain degree of self and mutual respect. But, in actuality the real reason I worked so hard to avoid getting into trouble at school was because I knew that if I did get in trouble my father would beat me like a Congo drum when I got home.

Dad's philosophy was clear. He told my teachers that if I acted up in school they could beat me there and he would beat me when I got home. If that was simply an idle threat to keep me scared straight, it worked.

I recall at Elementary School #1, where I attended, there were some rather odd ways that teachers and the principal dealt with kids who were less than cooperative in the area of behavior. It was not unusual while eating lunch in the cafeteria to see several school mates standing at the front of the room balancing on one leg.

There were four or five circles taped on the floor of the cafeteria up near the stage area. The idea was to have rebellious youngsters stand inside these circles on one leg. This would actually go on during the entire lunch period. Given my lifelong propensity for being awkward and clumsy, I had a deep seated fear of being made to stand in the circle on one leg. It would certainly have been a source of great entertainment for the rest of the kids in the cafeteria as they watched me bob and weave in a fruitless effort to stay balanced on one leg. I can imagine it would have been like watching a buffalo dance the tango.

No, I seemed very content to act like I had a reasonable amount of sense when I was attending elementary school. The behavioral deterrents offered by my father and the school administration seemed to work in terms of keeping me on my toes and fearful of the consequences of ignorant, heathen actions. Well, actually it worked well the first nine years of school. For some reason when I got into tenth grade I turned on like a drug-induced ape.

I cannot for the life of me understand why at the age of about 16, I suddenly found it necessary to transform into a poster child for "Morons, Inc." It was not as if Dad caved in under the pressure. As a matter of fact, the more rebellious and heathenistic my behavior became, the more confident Dad seemed to become about dealing with me. It was as if he rose to the occasion. Dad was like a warrior. The more he was challenged, the stronger he got. This was definitely not in my best interest.

I knew he was like a brick wall, yet time after time I would run at breakneck speed into his wrath. Dad had no patience with irreverent behavior from a young'un, but the most serious offense in his book was when we would "sass" or become disrespectful. I recall blatantly telling Dad one evening that I questioned his justification for expecting me to get a haircut. Dad was never in the mood for having diplomatic relationships with his kids. It was a dictatorship and Dad ruled. So, when I left Dad with the impression that I was not going to follow his orders and get a haircut, it was as if at that moment he began transforming into the Incredible Hulk. It started with his eyes. It seemed his eyes became enflamed with rage. He began breathing harder and his hands seemed to involuntarily clench.

He pushed himself up from the table and the chair he was sitting in flew across the kitchen floor like it was on ice. I am not sure if it was the dramatic scene that was unfolding in front of my eyes, or possible the fact that I knew with great certainty that Dad was about to roll me around the kitchen like a used tire, that caused me to recant my previous statement.

Just scant seconds before Dad pounced on me like a bobcat on a mule carcass; I threw up the white flag. At that moment I would have been willing to get up from the table and walk the seven miles to the barber. Without striking a single blow Dad made his point and got his desired results. Now, that is talent.

The virtue of having a big head

I always felt that growing up I was pretty normal. Oh yea, I am sure there would still be those who could happily point out that I was normal, except for the size of my head. I never thought that my head was larger than most; however, it was pointed out to me on numerous occasions. If that was not enough, you must remember that having a big head means you have to have a big face to cover it.

I am sure that in today's politically correct environment I could have easily had several people arrested for bullying when it came to rude remarks about my head size. I would probably have considered most of the comments to be no more than playful gestures from my immediate friends, but the comments oftentimes came from people I did not even know.

For instance, one day when I was about 13 or 14, I was walking down Columbia Avenue in my hometown of Crisfield, when I saw two young girls walking toward me. They were looking at me and whispering as I approached. I immediately became very excited because these cute girls seemed absolutely in awe of me. It was obvious that I was being tagged team with affection. These girls were so into me that I suddenly found myself for the first time in my young life, feeling somewhat cocky. This, I felt, was what it meant to be "hot."

The girls and I passed like ships in the night on that sidewalk. As they went past beside me I attempted my coolest, "hot guy" walk and look. Just as they went by I heard one girl say to other girl, "Did you see the size of his head; it was huge." Just last Wednesday I finally got over this episode and had the courage to write about it.

But, seriously, that hurt. Should there be any reason to question why I have always been so shy and in fear of rejection by members of the opposite sex? I think not.

I guess it would be bad enough to simply have a big head, but that unfortunately seems to go hand in hand with a thick neck. This resulted one day in someone who I felt was a great friend commenting about my head and neck. He made it clear to everyone within ear range that the last time he saw any living creature with a head and neck as big as mine was in a bull ring in Madrid.

I believe I have actually spent my adult life subconsciously allowing my weight to gain so as to enable my head to seem in proportion to the rest of my body. But, fear not those of you who possess large heads. Be proud and do not allow your head to be a burden, hanging down and creating unnecessary strain on your lower neck.

I feel that having a big head and thick neck have provided great opportunity for me over the years. For instance, few are the times that I was accidentally overlooked during a head count. I cannot recall anyone being able to borrow my favorite hat, except for the time it was used to tote tomatoes from the field when we ran out of bushel baskets. I have also never had to endure someone head-butting me during an act of jubilation.

I have been struck in the head with baseballs, rocks, sticks, the occasional shoe and more tree limbs than you could find in Redden Forest, yet never have I been seriously incapacitated. Of course we could never actually tell if my head had swollen during any of these instances.

Ok, enough about my big head. But, during this time of war, outrageous gas prices and sky rocketing food costs, if reading about the size of my head and the life of misery that has accompanied it, has caused you to at least smile it was worth exploiting my massive cranium.

Pictures do not lie. This is me at age 12.
There seems to be truth to the whole "big head" thing.

The sounds of my youth

I was riding down the road the other morning and began to think about sounds. This is certainly an unusual thought topic, I suppose. However, it amazes me that you can hear a classic song on the radio that may have been big during a certain time in your life and just the sound of that song can enable you to recreate the emotions and bring back the memories of that period of time.

So, I began to think about noises that I consider a part of my childhood. I truly believe if I heard these sounds I would automatically be catapulted back in time to my early years in Crisfield, Md. There is the sound of bottles clanging together. Not just any bottles, but Coca-Cola bottles being unloaded in front of Archie Tyler's store on Maryland Avenue. My childhood home was located at 209 Richardson Avenue, directly across the street from Archie's store. My bedroom was located upstairs and a window next to my bed faced the store. In the summertime our windows were open because for our family there was no such thing as air conditioning. I would wake to the sounds of those bottles ringing as they were unloaded from the truck and taken into the front door of the store.

I can close my eyes and see the inside of Archie Tyler's store; the dark, wooden floors and the walls full of merchandise. A rack to the right of the front counter was occupied by fruit pies, honey buns and my favorite, oatmeal cakes. Whenever I got a nickel I would run to Archie's and buy an oatmeal cake. When I could only muster up a few pennies I would buy what we called "pinwheels." These are the caramel candy with sugar cream in the middle. These were two for a penny. This was perfect nutrition for a young hoodlum. As if I did not have enough energy to wreak havoc on the neighborhood, I would eat these sugar infested oatmeal cakes with thick, oozing cream in the middle and top it off with caramel and sugar cream pinwheels. I am sure I was bouncing off the walls like a 10-cent store Superball.™

Then there was the sound of the ice cream truck. This was music to a young boy's ears. I couldn't hear Mom call me in for a bath from the backyard, but I could hear the ice cream truck bell and music from three counties away. I was fortunate that Mom loved the ice cream truck as much as we did. We would run to the house and my mother would be on the front porch digging through her coin purse and handing out the ice cream order. It was usually the same order a Nutty Buddy™ ice cream cone from Mom, a Fudgesicle™ for my grandmother and Popsicles™ for us young'uns. I always liked ice cream sandwiches, but if one of us got something more than a Popsicle™, there would be an ignorant display from the other brothers. So, Mom kept it simple.

Looking back I wonder how Mom could even stomach having one of us young'uns bringing the ice cream back home. I must have been a hideous sight walking the ice cream back to my Mom and grandmother. It never failed that I would have been outside playing in the dead heat of summer, sweating from head to toe and covered in two inches of dirt. I can imagine handing my mother her ice cream with a face covered in a mix of dirt and sweat, a dirt necklace around my neck and hands that were so dirty it looked like I was wearing gloves. However, this apparently did not deter my mother or grandmother because they ate the ice cream like it was about to be confiscated. Then there was the sound of the summer's most impressive recreational outlet – the mosquito truck. I am confident that when Somerset County sent the truck down to spray for mosquitoes in Crisfield, it was not part of their plan to provide a mobile playground for the Windsor young'uns. However, we certainly became creative at developing outlets for our playful energy. I could hear the loud, roar of the truck making its way down Richardson Avenue. There was a particularly recognizable sound as the operator let out a spray of thick, billowing insecticide that spread throughout the yards in the neighborhood. I would run to the curb and spy the billowing cloud of mosquito spray and fun was set in motion.

The mosquito spray truck was more important to us than even the ice cream truck. I would summon my brothers and all of my friends and we would hide behind the hedge and wait. We could hear the truck approaching and prayed that he waited until he was close to us before letting loose with the spray. The truck would go past and all at once the thick, billowing smoke cloud would spray out and we would take off like roaches in a lighted kitchen.

We would run into the street and dance in the cloud of carcinogenic smoke like retarded orangutans. I still recall how thick the smoke was and the pure awesome glory I experienced as I danced around in the cloud. I have often wondered why I did not develop some flesh-eating disease or why my son was not born with two heads. I guess there were no long term damages. However, I am not dead yet, so anything is possible.

Dad, a force to be reckoned with

He was a force to be reckoned with. There was no room for negotiations and his word was law. He was intimidating, he was smart and he operated with the life philosophy of a military strategist. He ranked just this side of God in terms of those people I did want to upset. He was Dad.

When it came to recreational outlets and social opportunities, I think being raised in Crisfield, Md. was not much different than spending your childhood in a wooden box buried beneath the ocean floor. Bottom line, there was not much to do in Crisfield during the 1960s and 1970s. What actually was accomplished were grand opportunities for me to excel as the village heathen.

As a young boy I learned through experience those things that could lead to a shortening of lifespan or the prospect of living my life in a physically disabled fashion. These included, but were not limited to, jumping out of the second-floor window of Mae Ford's vacant house onto a pile of mattresses, leaping off Miss Townsend's outhouse holding an umbrella, chucking clamshells during neighborhood war games held 10 o'clock at night, shoving an unusually large head into a street sewer drain in search of minnows, and making Dad angry. The most dangerous of these of course, was the latter.

I knew the potential for injury that came by making my father angry, but was drawn toward that goal like a monkey to a banana. You see, Dad was a man of action. He did not do a lot of talking. It was not his style to lecture you about what you had done wrong. He would rather demonstrate and use lots of visual aids. His lectures came while he was doling out the discipline, that way he had the opportunity to place proper emphasis on the points he wanted to make sure I was clear on.

Don't get me wrong, Dad was a wonderful husband, father and provider. He just would not take any crap. He crawled through the snow of Korea during the Korean Conflict where he commanded a unit as a sergeant in the U.S. Army. He took a bullet in the leg and was struck by shrapnel from a hand grenade. He broke up mayhem on the streets of Cambridge, Md. during the 1960s race riots, where he worked around the clock as both a member of the Army National Guard and the Maryland State Police. So, it should have been obvious to me at an early age that he was not about to let his life become uncomfortable due to the actions of a big-headed, knuckle-faced heathen like me.

But, I tended to ignore the obvious warning signs that pointed to Dad's anger level. Let me give just one of a score of examples of how stupid I was as a young'un. It was a hot, August afternoon. For some reason it seems that in Crisfield the summer brought heat like that in Africa and mosquitoes the size of a small airplane. Dad was high atop a ladder, beating off mosquitoes and painting the house. Now, I can assure you that Dad would just as soon been wrestling a wild boar as painting the house in mid-August.

This should have given me pause for thought and caused me to consider, at the very least, staying away from Dad's work area. But no, I had to hover directly under his ladder and commence to get into an argument with my younger brother. The argument turned to blows and I did the unthinkable; I let out with a curse word. Dad had certain rules of order in our household. One of the rules at the top of the list was that we young'uns were forbidden to curse. We were allowed to hear Dad curse, but we ourselves, could not curse.

Now, keep in mind, I had already heard Dad from where he was perched on the ladder warn me and my brother that he did not want to "come down off this ladder." But come down he did, and in quick fashion. Like a Ninja he was in my face and on me like ugly on an ape. I think he beat me all the way into the house and I don't think he even opened a door. To some this may sound harsh. But, one thing is for sure, I think Dad got the house painted without one single interruption and to my best recollection, I never uttered another curse word, at least not around Dad.

Cigars and a bomb threat

Dennis Morgan and I were tight. When I was about 15, the two of us were inseparable. It was the early 1970s when Dennis and I hung out together. He was a product of the 1960s complete with bell-bottom jeans, tie-dyed headband and no shoes. His record collection boasted Janis Joplin, Jimi Hendrix, John Prine and Simon and Garfunkel.

Dennis and I never wasted any time getting started on our journeys every weekend. First light of Saturday morning found us ready to head to the big city – Salisbury, Md. I remember one day Dennis and I and a couple of friends, Jimmy D. and Jimmy F., decided to head for the Salisbury mall where we would "hang out" until heading over to the store on Bateman Street where we would buy bootleg eight-track tapes.

These tapes were great. They only cost about $2. The titles of the songs and name of the bands were typewritten on the front of the tape. Sometimes the actual album cover would be photo-copied and stuck to the front of the tape.

I was lucky to listen to the complete tape once before it either stretched and broke, or began resembling the sound track from the exorcism scene in "The Exorcist."

It was obvious these tapes were bootleg because no matter what tape you got it was guaranteed that the tracks would run out before the songs did. Tracks two, three and four would always start in the middle of the song that was supposed to be the last song on the previous track.

So, anyway, this one day the four of us headed to the Salisbury Mall. When we got there we walked into the lobby and it was eerily desolate.

We noticed as we walked into the building there was a large crowd of people standing and milling around the parking lot. To anyone else this would have seemed unusual, but Jimmy F. had already rationalized that because it was the middle of December, it was obvious that the mall was planning its annual airlift of Santa Claus into the parking lot.

Any minute the bearded fellow would be parachuting down to the joy of the waiting crowd. So, being the typically ignorant corn-fed mules that we were, we went on into the mall, oblivious to the fact that "something was wrong here."

We walked into the area of the mall where the water fountain was located and the four of us sat on the edge of the fountain. Looking around we could see what appeared to be people in each of the stores bent down among the aisles of clothing, electronics and whatever else was being peddled.

These people moved quickly so it was difficult to see what they were doing. The one thing we did quickly realize was that we were definitely alone Out of the corner of my eye I saw the familiar shape of a dog. It was a huge German shepherd dog. I saw it attached to the end of a leash, sniffing under a counter in the McCrory's™ store. I followed the dog's leash back to a hand. The hand was attached to a rather rugged looking state trooper. It seems that we had walked into the mall during a bomb threat.

Police officers were everywhere, searching for potential explosive devices and there we sat like mice in a garden salad. Needless to say, we left the mall.

The ride home turned out to be what I will always consider as one of the worst days of my life. Dennis picked up a couple of packs of "fine" cigars on the way back to

Marion Station. It was the four of us in Dennis' yellow Rambler, a car just a few inches bigger than Barbie's Pink Camaro. We all lit up and began puffing. Seeking to appear "cool" I sucked on my cigar like an Oreck vacuum cleaner on a bowling ball.

By the time we got to Princess Anne, we couldn't see one another inside the car for the smoke. I began to feel like Grant's troops had pitched tents in my stomach. My stomach began to turn and churn like Mom's old wringer washer. I still to this day begin to break out in a sweat and feel nauseous just thinking about it. I was in such bad shape that all I could do was pray that prayer that we all have said at least once in our life, "Oh, dear Lord, if you will just get me over this, I will never smoke another cigar."

When we pulled into the driveway at my house, my good friends opened the door and pushed me out onto the ground like a bag of mail. I lay there looking up at the stars, dreading the long crawl up the front steps.

It was truly misery, but you know what? I never did smoke another cigar.

Living tomorrow's 'good old days'

I often question whether "the good old days" are actually any better than the present days. I sometimes think maybe they just seem better because they have passed by and do not impact our daily living. I am sure "the good old days" included hardships, disappointments, struggles and miseries just like the days of present. But, we tend to exclude some of those more negative aspects when we recall these bygone days.

I am certainly prone to nostalgia and find reminiscing to be a welcome relief to the challenges of my daily life. I realize that when I think back on the days of my youth the sun seemed to shine brighter, the grass was greener, the breeze was so much cooler in the summer and the house was toasty warm during the bitter winter. I want to see if I can recall my youth more accurately and in a less than "rose-colored glasses" image.

The Crisfield home I lived in as a child was demolished shortly after we left it in 1970. I'm not saying our landlord was glad to see us finally leave, but I think we were still packing when the bulldozers started pushing in the walls. None the less, the home went down and a new home was built on the property within a year.

I recently went back to my childhood home place. For the first time in 35 years I actually did more than drive past the property. I stopped my van in front of what in 1969 would have been the front porch of my home. Today there is a small, attractive bungalow where my home once stood.

As I looked into the yard that my brothers and I once played in; it seemed extraordinarily smaller. This led me to my next conclusion. Since it is impossible that the land mass shrunk, I must be extraordinarily bigger. The backyard that in my childhood memories seemed to expand for miles, was no more than a patch of grass, maybe 15 or 20 yards in width and length.

The hedge that separated our house from our neighbor "Miss Addie," is still there. However, it must have shrunk because it is at least four feet shorter than I recall it being when I was 10 years old. Oh, that's right; I have not only gotten wider, but taller as well. So, perhaps the hedge is really the same size.

I looked down at the street that ran past my house and sure enough, there was the storm drain that was my childhood fishing hole. I can vividly recall bending down over the iron grates that covered the drain and sticking my head and hands down into the opening at the back. I would clench bread between my fingers and catch minnows.

How in the world did I get my head in that small opening? Even as a child my head could have easily been compared to a #10 wash bucket. I almost immediately had a flash back of the day when at the age of about 5-years-old, a man driving down Richardson Avenue spied me hunched over with my head shoved down in the drain.

Now, I would ask anyone to rationalize that experience from the perspective of that motorist. He had to figure I was either on my way down the sewer hole, on my way back out, or more likely, my head was stuck in the storm drain. So, as any "Good Samaritan", would do, he pulled over and ran over to me. Huffing and puffing, he grabbed me like a sack of fresh picked sweet potatoes. He then placed one arm around my waist while using the other hand to cradle my head, and commenced pulling me up.

I was not stuck, I was fishing. But, up came me and about six minnows that I had caught previously, as well as one clenched between my fingers. As my mother came out the front door the man was holding me, safe and sound. He proudly announced to my mother than he was riding by and saw me with my head stuck in the storm drain. My mother, for the first time possibly in my young life, actually took a hard look at me, assessed the size of my head and found the man's story very believable.

But, back to the point of my column; standing on what to me is holy ground, I found myself overwhelmed by sentimentality, as I looked out over my old neighborhood. Even though another structure stood in place of my childhood home, in my mind I could still see every room, and nook and cranny of my childhood home. I saw the steps that led to the porch, the door that led to the living room, the stairs that led to our upstairs bedrooms and the morning gathering place called the kitchen.

I could see the living room floor where as a child I lay in front of the black and while television watching "Lassie." This was also the location of more than one confrontation with my father. This because he would barely walk through the front door after work and be hit with a status report from my mother regarding my heathen behavior for the last 10 hours. So, the very spot where I was once lying in front of the television, I could now be found rolling around in the floor like a legless dog trying to dodge my dad's belt.

It amazes me how clearly I can recreate my entire childhood home in my mind, literally every square inch of it. I realize that this is because it is part of the "good old days" and something that represents security and most importantly, family. As I stood on that spot in Crisfield where every morning as a child I would bolt out the door and welcome a new day, I realized a lot had changed. But, I also realized that while the environment changed and things were not as they were when I was a child, everything was still the same where it counted – in my mind and my memories of the "good old days."

Thawing pipes was a 'Dad's jobs'

I read recently where a man in Massachusetts used a blow torch to melt the ice that had formed on the porch of his home. The end result was $35,000 damages to his home after he set it on fire with the torch.

As I read the article I was reminded of the many times my father would crawl under our house with a propane torch and work to melt the ice that had formed in the water lines depriving us of household water.

I can still see Dad scrunched up under the house, barely enough room to breathe, running the flame of the torch up and down the frigid water pipe. The flame of the torch would be just inches from the wood floor of the kitchen, which was as dry as a powder horn. Our entire house was like a tinder box, primed and ready to go up like a Homecoming bonfire at the first contact of a spark of loose ash.

I find it amazing and extremely fortunate, that we never suffered a fire at that old monstrosity we called home. There was room to crawl under our house and the foundation was wide open to the elements. I can still remember in the summertime while we were outside playing we would know when Mom was doing dishes because you could see the soapy water running out of the pipe under the house. It was an environmental hazard, I suppose, but it sure made it easy to retrieve the silverware and dish rags that would sometimes get sucked down the sink drain.

Having the foundation of the house open left us vulnerable to the winter weather. Whenever "Old Man Winter" cast his frigid breath over Crisfield we could be sure to have frozen water pipes.

I was a young boy, so it only meant that I would not have access to water from the kitchen sink when the pipes froze. To Dad this meant a great deal more. He would throw on his winter coat, get the propane torch and crawl under the house like a coal miner. Of course I would have to go out and hunker down beside the house to watch him do his makeshift plumbing work. This was not because I was necessarily excited to assist my father in his "grownup" chore, but more because it involved a lit flame. Something about fire drew young'uns like moths.

I can see my father like it was yesterday. He would be packed in so tight under the house that you couldn't get a piece of paper between him and the floor of the house. Then he would have to contort his arms in order to bring the propane torch up to the pipe. It was a grueling job. I have to imagine his arms ached after doing what would sometimes be over an hour of thawing pipes. I would watch as Dad would run the flame up and down the pipe, hoping to suddenly hear rushing water. But, this was a "Dad job" and had to be done.

The other half of the job included replacing the insulation wrap that Dad kept around the pipes. This tended to work unless we had bitter cold weather. I also recall Dad using the electric insulation wraps, which involved extension cords and again, a dry, brittle house foundation. Our house was old and was nothing more than a big stack of structured kindling wood.

But, it is really weird how much I have missed that old house throughout my adult life. Snow would blow in through the cracks in our bedroom windows and pile up on the floor and when the wind blew the rattling doors and windows sounded like someone running through the middle of the house.

I can't recall a winter where the living room stove ever ran for longer than a day or two without breaking down. Dad had to work on the stove so many times he left the front panel leaning up against the wall all winter just to keep from having to take it off each time.

We had one cold water pipe that supplied water to the kitchen and no indoor bathroom, but even though I have lived in my current house for over 30 years, I still consider that old Crisfield monstrosity "home."

Dad's threats were almost poetic

I was thinking the other day about how my father seemed to have a knack for making a point with his little phrases that are now synonymous with my memories of him. For instance, never was the time I got a dime from Ira Lowe the barber after a haircut that Dad wouldn't say, "I guess that dime is going to burn a hole in your pocket before you can spend it." I never really understood what that meant, but it was obvious that it was Dad's reference to my pacing the floor until I could get to Bryan Hall's store and buy something.

When I was acting more like a circus clown on crack than someone with his right mind, Dad would make it clear that he was not far from , "Knocking me seven ways from Sunday," or "knocking me into next week." That was a mental visual that created pause for reflection.

If I ever asked Dad where he was going when he headed out the door, I could always count on him saying, "Crazy, and you're driving me there." Or any other question that I had that Dad did not care to answer, he would simply ask, "Are you writing a book? Leave that chapter out." Now I know that today these phrases are worn out, but you have to remember to a young boy who hung on every word his father said, it was as if my father was the cleverest human being in the universe.

If I was late getting home, I was always "lollygagging," and if I took too long to answer one of his questions I was "hem hauling." I wonder if anybody actually knows what these two terms are, or where they got their origin?

If I got in trouble at school, I could count on Dad to point out that, "You think the rest of the world is out of step." I think in that case he was pretty much right on the money. If I promised Dad I would take care of some chore, which most generally I would wind up "hem hauling" or "lollygagging" prior to getting around to it, he would say, "Don't tell me what you're gonna do, do it and tell me what you done."

Amazingly enough, the words that I seem to remember the most and which have been advice that I use in many of life's situations has nothing to do with life or any of its situations. It comes from what Dad would say every time he would get me and my brother to help pen up some ducks or geese that had gotten out of their compound. They were very flighty and easily scared when we would approach to coax them back into their confines.

Dad would have us form a half-circle and slowly with outstretched arms we would head toward the flock of fowl. Dad's same advice would come every time without fail, "Slow down, don't rush 'em, take it easy, move slow." I find that this is advice that works in most every decision-making or stressful situation in life. I think most people in the world would do well to, "Slow down. Don't rush. Take it easy and move slow." Of course in reality, because he was dealing with young'uns who could never do anything in a structured, disciplined manner, those very wise and judicious words would come from Dad just moments before he followed them up with some other sincere offerings, most usually, "You're rushing 'em! You're getting 'em scared! Get the hell in the house; I'll do it my damn self!"

Money burned a hole in my pocket

There it was. I could hardly believe it. Lying half covered in the dirt was a shiny round object. Closer inspection confirmed my greatest expectations; it was a quarter. A quarter may not sound like much, but when you are nine years old in 1966, it was like finding a brick of gold.

Before I even managed to pick it up I started imagining where and how I would spend it. I had it spent by the time I got it in hand. When you received money, whether the 10-cents our barber Ira Lowe always gave us after a haircut, or the 25-cents my grandmother would give me for helping her during the week, there was certain criteria to follow. If it was less than a dollar you would go to Archie Tyler's or Bryan Hall's stores to spend it. If it was more than a dollar, it was off to McCrory's™ (the 10-cent store). Once I had the quarter in my pocket I tore off for town like Grant through Richmond. Mr. Archie's store was my family's "Food Lion." If I was craving candy or Oatmeal cakes, or maybe those chocolate cupcakes with white cream inside, that is where I would go. However, if had my mind a toy then it was off to Bryan Hall's store. Walking into Bryan Hall's store I would scan the rows of candy neatly stacked against the front counter and then look at the spinning metal rack that contained all kinds of gimmicks and gadgets. I had gotten every item at one time or another.

There was the stink bomb. That was a riot. I small ball with a fuse that once lit would eventually emit a smoke cloud of gaseous sulfur. Why was that legal? Even more importantly, what possible use could there be for anyone other than a juvenile delinquent?

There was the small buzzer that you could use to shake hands with somebody and deliver a buzzing vibration in the palm of their hand. This seemed like such a clever and humorous practical joke. But, given the fact that I can recall maybe once in my childhood that I shook hands with one of my friends it was hard to set up the joke.

I would walk up to one of my friends with hand stretched out and say, "Hey, shake hands." There was hardly an element of surprise. I would have been more successful if I had been wearing a sandwich board proclaiming I had just been to Bryan Hall's and had bought a handshake buzzer.

Of course I could always buy paper caps. They were normally reserved for the cap pistol I would get each year for Christmas. However, by summertime I was lucky if there was a trigger or barrel left to the gun. But, I would still buy paper caps. There would be anywhere from three to six rolls of paper caps depending on the price.

I would take the caps home and sit down on the back porch steps with a brick and a hammer. If I didn't have access to a hammer, another brick would do. I would take the roll of paper caps and slam a brick down on top of it and hear the loud crack of the miniature explosion, watching as the smoke and gunpowder shot out from the impact. This would last between two and four minutes, depending on whether I had three or six rolls of paper caps.

Looking back on this exercise in futility it is easy to see I was certainly no ball of creative energy. More often than not, I would wind up buying the little Army man that was attached to a parachute. He was green, dressed in fatigues and holding a rifle. The plastic parachute was with him, folded strategically inside the cellophane package. The outside of the bag stated, "Hours of fun. Watch this military hero float down for action anywhere you choose." What action? He was a hollow soft plastic replica of a soldier. But, I would buy it and run home to play with it. The first thing I had to do was untangle the six to eight threads that attached the parachute to the soldier. I would then throw the soldier high in the air and watch him float down.

I would then pick him up, untangle the six to eight threads and throw him again. It was probably six times in the air before the threads would either break one at a time or get so tangled I would grow impatient trying to straighten them out. Eventually the parachute would only open about half way because the strings were tangled and the soldier would fall like a soft rock.

It would be 30 minutes into my play with the parachuting soldier that I would usually send him on his last mission; to parachute into the burning barrel of trash my dad would have set a few minutes earlier. Including the time it took to get to the store, pick out the toy, run back home and play with the soldier, that quarter I found had given me an hour of entertainment. I would just need to figure out what to do with the other eight or nine hours I had before bedtime.

Not many trips to the hospital

It is officially football season. I am not a big football fan, but those people who are become extraordinarily manic about this time of year. I remember growing up where my high school in Crisfield did not have a football program. We had soccer, basketball, softball and field hockey.

I can only imagine we had no football because it was such a contact sport. I am thinking that having some Crisfielder out on a field with a license to trounce someone would be a liability nightmare. I fear our athletes may have taken the idea of contact sports a bit too far. They would probably have been the only football team to show up on the field with baseball bats. Of course I jest. But, I always remember baseball being my favorite sport as I was growing up. This reminds me of a rather unpleasant memory of baseball in my neighborhood.

I can't shake it. The sound has stayed with me, hidden inside my head for the last 45 years. It was the dull thud of my softball bat striking my best friend in the forehead. No, it was not an act of intentional violence. We were playing ball in the backyard of my home and my friend, Carey, was crouched in the catcher's position behind me as I batted.

Apparently, he moved too far forward, or I moved too far backwards and as I swung the bat to make a powerful swat at the oncoming pitch I made early contact with Carey's head. It is just like an hour ago. I can still feel the bat reverberate and the sound as it slammed into his ample forehead. It was much like the feel of a bat should you swing and strike it against an oak tree. I immediately turned in horror and watched as Carey's forehead began to swell until it looked as if he were giving birth to a second head.

A knot the size of a large goose egg was sticking out from the front of his head, just above his eyes. My response to this tragic event was much like that which would have come had I stumbled upon "Big Foot." I said, "Oh, man! That is huge!"

Now, certainly having just been slammed with a baseball bat across the forehead, Carey must have been knocked out and been left totally immobilized. Not so. Carey covered his newly acquired head ornament and stumbled off home. Surely his parents rushed him to the hospital for fear of concussion? Not so. Carey returned a few minutes later sporting a cold, wet cloth across his forehead and even ditched that within 15 minutes. Our day of play continued as if nothing happened.

I am not condoning this less than enthusiastic reaction to Carey's blow to the head; perhaps he should have gotten precautionary medical treatment. I mean it is not every day that you have your forehead pummeled with a wooden bat. But, the truth is, when I was growing up unless there was some evidence of potentially lost limbs or eyes, we did not go to the doctor or, God forbid, the hospital.

It was not that our parents cared less about us. It was simply that years ago most medical treatment was administered by family. If I stepped on a nail, which I seemed to do at least once or twice a summer, or slashed my bare foot on a broken bottle, the remedy was soaking the wound in a basin of salt water. Of course every cut no matter how significant was always treated with Methylate or Mercurochrome™. These two topical antiseptic treatments were pink in color and one would sting more than the other, but I could never remember which one hurt the worse. So, as

Mom approached with the small, dark-colored bottle I would begin to cry and beg for her to avoid this step in the treatment process. She would assure me that this would not sting and for me not to worry. So, as she applied the solution I learned quickly that she had lied to me. But, in traditional mother style she would blow on the wound to help cool the sting. I always thought that was kind of neat.

But, we rarely went to a doctor for treatment. Today children, including my own son when he was a child, go to the emergency room or doctor's office at the first cough or sneeze. I think with the availability of air conditioning and other modern day conveniences, our children are more susceptible to illness and in some ways are not as rugged as we were as kids. I can actually remember the times I was taken to a doctor or the hospital from time I was born until I left home at 17. There were a total of three such visits in my childhood.

One was at the age of about 10 when I was attacked by a Chesapeake Bay Retriever and had to be given 30 stitches to me chest area. There was the time that I had a particularly extensive case of poison ivy that totally covered my back and I had to visit Dr. Sarah Peyton's office. Then there was the time I failed to call a baseball catch and collided with the center fielder and fractured my finger. The remaining childhood infirmities, including measles, mumps, chicken pocks, whooping cough, the Asian Flu, nails in the feet, bats to the head and one incident in which I ran headlong into a parked pickup truck, all were maintained at home under the care of either nurse Mom or surgeon Dad.

I made it through my childhood, so whether by design or accident, I suppose my parents knew best when it came to health issues. At least I think they did.

Color TV for $1.98?

The black and white television in my childhood living room received a grand total of one station on a regular basis. WBOC-TV16 was only one of two sources of entertainment for the Windsor family. The other source of entertainment was watching Dad adjust the manually controlled TV antenna in an attempt to view a Baltimore of Philadelphia TV station. We had a television antenna on our roof and a contraption on top of the television with a bar that controlled the direction of the antenna. At night we would use the dial and try to pick up a station from out of state.

I would be amazed when on a clear summer night we watched shows like "The Green Hornet," "Batman," "Zorro," "Have Gun Will Travel," or maybe even "Chiller" or "The Twilight Zone."

Of course half the show would be spent spinning the antenna around on the roof like a tank turret, trying to get a good signal when the television screen began to get snowy. When you were not used to anything but one channel, even snowy, distorted pictures seemed somewhat of a luxury. I can also remember times when the antenna control would break and Dad would be watching "Combat" or a John Wayne movie, and he would scale the house and climb on top of the roof and manually twist the antenna.

It was like a communications bucket brigade as Dad would be on the roof with one of us kids at the nearest window shouting; the remaining family members stationed all the way back to the television. Dad would twist the antenna and wait as he would get affirmation from the line crew that he was going in the right direction. This would go on until either we got the best available picture or Dad got fed up with our unwillingness to settle for either, ripples, ghosts or snow, or a combination of all three.

It never failed that by the time he would climb back down off the roof and get in front of the TV, the wind would change and the reception would be gone again.

But, we could pretty much count on Channel 16 to come through. So, we were entertained with nightly news from John B. Greenberger, weather from Nancy Pigman and the nightly Curly Cues trivia question hosted by Ralph Pennewell and sponsored by Curley's clothing store.

Benjamin's, another popular Salisbury clothing store also outfitted Nancy Pigman in the latest styles as she did the nightly weather report. Following the report she would do a fashion show promoting Benjamin's clothing lines. But, there was more to Channel 16 then simply the local fare. Sunday nights brought us "Mister Ed," "Lassie," "The Wonderful World of Disney," "Bonanza" and "The Sunday Night Movie."

I would never have believed there would be a day when you could bring a movie home and watch it on a round, silver disc. By the time a movie got to Crisfield's Arcade Movie Theater, most of the actors had died and it had become a classic.

There were those special times of the year when we would gather around the television to watch such annual favorites as "The Wizard of Oz," "The Robe" and of course the one commercial that made us aware that Christmas was truly close....Santa Claus sliding down the hill on the Norelco Electric Razor. But, everything we watched was in black and white. This was frustrating because some of my friends were starting to get color televisions. I recall the night they announced that The Wizard of Oz would be telecast with the first half of the movie in black and white and the last half in color. I could only imagine what those horrible little flying monkeys might have looked like in color. Commercials soon started touting the Zenith color TV. It was pure magic to consider a television that could actually show colors.

About this same time somebody started selling a product that they claimed would turn a black and white television into a color TV. I found the product at the "10-Cent Store (McCrory's™)" in downtown Crisfield and being almost as intelligent as a turnip, I bought it. It cost $1.98 and I rushed home with it like I was carrying a bag filled with the cure for cancer.

I opened the package and it turned out to be a sheet of plastic that was to be taped over the television screen. The plastic sheet was tri-colored. Horizontally across the top was tinted blue, the middle of the sheet was a light gold and the bottom of the plastic sheet was tinted green. The idea was that while watching a television show, the sky would be blue and the grass green, in the middle would be tinted just enough to have some sense of color.

So, while watching a show, like say, "Bonanza," as the Cartwrights were traveling horseback to Virginia City, the sky was indeed blue and the grass green. Of course when they were in the kitchen with Hop Sing, the ceiling was also blue and the floor green. As a matter of fact when Hoss was pitching hay in the barn the loft was blue and the stable was green. So, it was obvious that I had been taken early on by deceptive advertising. Of course, if I had possessed a brain commensurate with the size of my head, I would have figured this product out long before I bought it. Oh well, I guess the early days of television saw me coming with the egg money. I am sure little has changed in that respect.

It was only a year or so later that my dad bought us a color television set. I am not sure if that was the soonest he could afford it, or if that was when he finally stopped laughing.

What you don't know can hurt you!

He moved across the kitchen table with grace, silence and stealth. I was the only person who saw him make his way toward the freshly baked sweet potato pies. Once standing directly over the pies he suddenly leaned down and licked his velvet tongue across each of the three pies, one at a time.

I sat motionless staring into the kitchen as our big orange tomcat licked each of the three pies as if he was marking his territory. None of the family who was visiting our home for the holidays was aware that the cat had molested the pies in such a fashion.

Dinner time came and went and when everyone sat down for desert, I had the obligation to tell them what I had witnessed. There was my grandmother, Uncle Oscar and Aunt Evelyn laughing and joking with Uncle Coulbourn and Aunt Stella. Mom was her usual jovial, helpful hostess, serving up fresh tea as Dad began to slice the pie.

It was a scene out of a Norman Rockwell painting. It was Americana at its finest. How could I ruin this picturesque moment with news that the cat had licked the pies. I had a small window of opportunity to make my decision. I looked down at the floor and the cat had one leg lifted and was giving himself a bath. "My gawd, there is no way I can let them eat the pies that the cat licked," I thought to myself. As Dad passed out the pie he had sliced I gave it one more consideration and then went back to watching television, distracted at times from the joviality of the family dinner taking place in the next room.

Never did I hear anyone remark that the pies had any added flavor, or even that they were anything less than my mother's traditionally grand offerings. However, my father, Aunt Evelyn, Uncle Oscar, Uncle Coulbourn and Aunt Stella have since died. I hope there is no correlation.

The sad thing is, the cat licking the pie was not the only time that I recall hiding the truth when it came to nutritional health hazards. There was the family get together that necessitated my being sent across the street to Archie Tyler's store for some luncheon meats. Archie's store was the equivalent to today's Royal Farms store. Mr. Archie sliced his lunch meat from huge rolls of meat and on this particular day Mom asked me to get a mixture of bologna, cloth ham and honey ham.

I watched as Mr. Archie sliced the meats, wrapped them and neatly tied them with the white string that dangled from the ceiling attached to a large spindle. I threw down a nickel and purchased a handful of Mary Jane candy and headed off for home.

As I walked on the porch of my home I wrestled with the Mary Jane candy wrapper which had become attached to the candy like wallpaper. My fingers became so intent on getting to the candy that I lost focus on the three pounds of lunch meat I held in my arms. Suddenly the candy wrapper broke free and my fingers got caught up in the neatly tied lunch meat string. The lunchmeat flew out of my arms and all of the meat slid out of the stiff, white wrapping paper.

I looked down in horror as I saw bologna and cloth lunchmeat scattered at my feet. I quickly looked around to assure that no one had seen this tragedy unfold. I grabbed the lunch meat, most of which was speckled from the granules of dirt that were picked up off the porch floor. Some pieces I wiped clean as best I could with my hand.

Others, which had ground in dirt attached, I rubbed across the rough surface of my cotton shirt. I shoved the meat into the white paper and frantically retied the string. I went into the house and plopped the lunch meat down on the kitchen table and retreated to my bedroom.

As far as I know everyone had sandwiches and reveled in joy unrivaled by recent family reunions. As best I can tell, though the aforementioned individuals have since died, there were no casualties from the dirty lunch meat. So, I suppose there may be some merit to the age-old phrase, "What you don't know, won't hurt you."

When opposites finally attract

I often wonder why my parents always seemed to dote on my older brother. It was as if he held the secret to world peace. Perhaps it was just sibling rivalry, but I guess I grew up being jealous of my brother. Looking back on the issue now, I realize that the reason my parents seemed to share so much affection for my brother was because he failed to get in as much trouble as I did.

Consequently, when my brother was being praised for another straight "A" report card, I was being punished for trying to hide my report card from my father. I used to hate being the child who came immediately after my older brother. I would see the faces of teachers light up when they saw that I was in the classroom that school year. After all, they had taught my brother two years earlier and found him to be "simply delightful."

I was expected to live up to the legacy left by my brother. NOT! This was a chore that I did not accept gracefully. I guess if we analyze this it would be easy to reach the conclusion that my misbehavior and failure to achieve in the classroom came from my desire to be the exact opposite of my brother. Forget that psychoanalytical stuff, the bottom line is I was a heathen. I somehow gained a sense of esteem from being the child everyone hated to see coming.

Dad only made my attitude worse when after reviewing my report card he would say, "It would be different if you were not as smart your brother. Then I would expect so much less from you. But the truth is you are smarter than your brother."

Man, how I hated to hear that analogy. I know Dad felt it his paternal duty to fill me with this type of support, but that just seemed to compel me to new heights of mayhem. As a matter of fact, now that I think about it, I believe it was just after one of those father-to-son talks that I was accused of chucking a handful of rocks through the open window of a passing city police car. This while waiting in the school parking lot for my bus ride home. The truth is that incident was perpetrated by the young man standing behind me. However, my innocence gave me the fuel to initiate a scene that had not been matched since Attica, when the policeman approached me to make an arrest. My cries of "police brutality" and "excessive force" could be heard miles away and created mass mayhem in the parking lot.

The school assistant principal appeared and seeing the need to take immediate action to calm the crowd, he convinced the police officer to allow him to deal with me. The officer agreed and once more I was in the principal's office hearing about the number of days I would be suspended from school. Also once again, I gave Mom and Dad every reason to support renting me out to the military for target practice.

The years have passed now I see things in a much different light. I no longer possess a jealousy in regard to my brother. He is an information technology specialist with the Arlington School District in Virginia, and as in the past, is quite the brain. However, as fate would have it, my brother recently collapsed on the streets of Arlington and was rushed to the hospital, where he underwent open-heart surgery. So, more than ever I realize that life takes in no consideration of our wealth of knowledge or our irreverent behavior when striking us with problems.

However, having undergone open-heart surgery myself two years ago, I could not resist telling my brother as he was recuperating in the hospital that I was sensitive to his plight. However, I had to throw in the fact that I had "been there, and done that." For once I had accomplished something major before my brother.

*Those were the eyes that seemed to look into
my soul. This was my father. This was my hero*

The eyes of Dad

His eyes would pierce through me like a knife through
butter. It was amazing that one man would have so much
effect on me. I idolized my father and considered him in my
mind's eye to be the greatest man to ever live. However, I
feared him like the Grim Reaper. I realize today as an adult,
Dad's talent to intimidate was no accident, he did it by
design.

As a police officer Dad used his ability to intimidate
whenever he stopped vehicles for speeding or caught a
young person drinking a beer. He operated in a time when
police officers were allowed discretion and did not have to
be motivated by mandated quotas. Dad could give a

speeding motorist a warning yet leave the driver truly repentant for his violation. It was all in the eyes.

Dad's eyes were no different than most. They were hazel in color, just like mine. His eyes were certainly not larger or in any other manner overpowering in size. I guess you could have actually called them small. No, it was not the eyes alone that created intimidation, but more the way Dad used them.

If we young'uns got into trouble at school or anywhere else in the neighborhood, we had little chance to keep it from Dad. There was a network in our small Crisfield and Marion Station communities that operated somewhat like the streets of Washington. In Washington all streets lead to the White House, in our town, all communication led to Dad.

In the event of those few instances when Dad had not heard about our heathen behavior by the time we walked in the door that afternoon or night, there was still one more detection device that went into action; that of course being the eyes. Dad had the uncanny ability to look into our eyes to detect our deceit. It was like interrogation under a hot light, only less dramatic. Dad simply asked us a question then stated that he would look into our eyes to see if we were telling the truth. At that time in my life there was no doubt in my young mind that Dad could truly read my mind by staring into my eyes. It was hopeless.

I knew there was no sense in lying because Dad would see, so I would always fess up within 10 seconds. I remember vividly that my youthful antics, which oftentimes involved heathen behavior, would be met with Dad's wrath. I had the ability to bring on the immediate, less tactful responses from my father; sometimes results that involved me being beat like a stuck lid on a jelly jar.

However, I recognize that my dad's success at discipline among his trio of retarded apes came not only from what my brothers and I knew Dad would do, but even more from what we feared he might do. Thus, those squinting, piercing eyes were many times all Dad had to use to bring us to full attention. How I dreaded to look into those eyes when I knew I had done something ignorant and offensive a few hours earlier.

Now, many years later, I am able to reflect and know that those eyes were a lot more than tools of intimidation. They were many times filled with pride over the accomplishments of one of his children, appreciation when looking at his wife, or sadness at the loss of someone he loved. Those eyes were sometimes tainted by frustration, but always filled with love. Now, I would give almost anything to look into the eyes of Dad.

My patience is limited at holidays

With Thanksgiving behind us, we now officially start the Christmas holidays. I really enjoy walking through the stores and viewing the elaborate holiday decorations. In the evening it is heartwarming to see the brightly decorated homes bursting with the spirit of the season.

I have never been one to take the necessary time to decorate my home. It is a matter of patience and this is something of which I have very little. I recall one Christmas I decided I would not have a Christmas tree. Then I found myself staring into the face of my very disappointed nine-year-old son. Needless to say, I had to make a last minute trip to the store to find a tree to decorate.

I found a four and a half-foot tall pine tree and dutifully set it up in the living room. This must have been a particularly depressing Christmas, because I recall holding the string of lights in one hand, grabbing the tree by the top branches, and spinning it around and around until the lights were tangled into every branch. I picked up the roll of garland and threw it around the tree like Roy Rogers roping a calf. I took the silver icicles by the fistful and threw them at the tree. As I hung ornaments on the tree and came across those balls which had no hooks, I would simply stick the balls in between branches. I had about as much Christmas spirit as Genghis Khan.

I think I managed to put on a happy face and get through Christmas for the sake of my son. When I finally got around to taking the tree down, which I think was March, I found myself facing an even tougher challenge. I began taking ornaments and those hideous icicles off the tree. However, when it came to taking the Garland and lights off, I found that because I have placed them on the tree so haphazardly, they had become entangled; a brain surgeon could not have cut them out. I struggled and every tug gave way to a sigh of desperation. I became so enraged that I grabbed the tree, lights, garland and all, and ran with it. I headed through the living room and dining room and on into the kitchen. I open the basement door and without even blinking, I chucked that albatross down into the black abyss.

It is sad to admit that I allowed myself to become so grim during such a beautiful holiday. However, I must confess that I look forward as much to tree trimming as I would to having my gallbladder taken out with a soup spoon.

I always pull a Tom Sawyer when it comes to decorating the tree. I find people who enjoy doing this task, or I would have a Christmas tree sitting in my living room that was as empty as the surface of the moon. I have noticed during my holiday jaunts to the stores that I must not be the only person with problems getting lights on the tree, because they are now offering pre-lit trees. I would buy one of those, except it would be a waste of money. After all, I have one of those still lying down the basement; believe it or not!

A lot like flying, except no wings

I had someone stop me last week and accuse me of making up the things that I write about in my columns. I assured her, and I assure you, that the accounts I share in my columns are actual occurrences. Not that my life's experiences really matter in the scheme of life, I mean, who cares? But, I do enjoy writing about these experiences because it allows me to stroll through the past and relive some of the more humorous moments.

I encourage everyone to do this whenever possible. You would he surprised how many pleasant memories you can bring to light. For example, I recall when my best friend Carcy moved out of Crisfield and his grandmother's house was left vacant. Many of the neighborhood heathens, of which we had a surplus, went into the house and pretty much trashed it.

My brothers and I went to the upstairs bedroom and threw three old bed mattresses out the window. They landed on the ground about 50-feet below and my older brother, Tommy, and I were immediately hit with an incredible idea Let's chuck our six- year-old brother, Jeff, out the window and see if we can get him to land on the mattresses.

Yes! Yes! Excitement rang throughout the room; perhaps not as much for my brother, Jeff, as for 'Tommy and me, but excitement nonetheless. So, out the window Jeff flew, arms flaying about, mouth gaped open. He landed on the mattresses below, rolled off and immediately jumped about, reveling in his newfound adventure.

After being assured that the venture was indeed successful, thanks to our live test dummy, Tommy and I decided we would make the flight. My brother, being the oldest, commanded my respect, so I allowed him to go first.

He leaned out the window and due to a sudden burst of intimidation, hesitated to make the leap.

I love my brothers. This was my oldest brother and I felt it important to support him when he was caught in the midst of fear, so I came up behind him and pushed him out the window. Not to worry. He landed safely on the pile of mattresses below. Now, it was my turn. I crawled up into the windowless frame and looked below. Suddenly I felt bad that I had shoved my two brothers out the window, mainly because they were now on their way back up the stairs.

Their angry banter and shouts of threatened retribution left me realizing that if I didn't jump on my own, I would certainly be forcefully plummeted out the window when they arrived in the bedroom. Worse yet, they were threatening to throw me out a different window.

Much like someone who is about to climb into a swimming pool and face the frigid water, I leaned out the window, then back in the window, then out the window again, trying various positions before mustering the courage to jump.

Finally, I had my incentive. As my brothers barreled into the bedroom like two gorillas in a Tarzan movie, I leaped out the window. Within what seemed to be a split second later, I landed abruptly on the mattresses. It was at that moment that I realized that my brothers had "accidentally" pulled two of the three mattresses off the pile. After initial jumps the fears subsided and leaping out the window became a passion for us all. This passion was short-lived however, when a friend of my father's from Cambridge, Md., came to visit our family one day.

As he drove down Richardson Avenue toward our house, he looked off to the right and what he saw took his breath away. The other houses that sat along the avenue in front of the house we were playing in somewhat obstructed the view.

As he looked in horror, all he could see was my younger brother, Jeff, leaping out the second story window, followed shortly thereafter by my brother Tommy and finally, me. He had no idea there were mattresses on the ground below, He must have thought we had made a suicide pact.

Needless to say, once my father learned of our new recreational activity, it was closed on the spot. It still amazes me that we were never hurt during our many leaps out that window. Today, either one of us would probably break a leg if we fell off a street curb.

Oh well, chalk it up to the follies of youth.

Band-Aids are not the best toy

I thought it was cool at the time. I envisioned that taking a box of Band-Aids™ and placing each strip strategically over different places on my face would result in the perfect impersonation of an Indian out of the old West. It looked great as I gazed in the mirror as if I were "Sitting Bull" or "Geronimo" about to go on the warpath.

However, off to the left side of the mirror, behind my head, I caught the reflection of my mother who upon seeing me using up a new box of Band-Aids™ to play cowboys and Indians was now herself ready for war. I reacted so quickly that the one thing I forgot to do was use common sense. I jumped out of the chair I was standing on and bolted out of the backdoor like I was being chased by Satan; Mom dead on my heels.

I ran around the side of the house and started heading down Richardson Avenue like Grant through Richmond. I imagined there was no way that my mother at the old age of 27, could possibly keep up with me at the spry age of five. I looked back over my shoulder and sure enough, Mom was matching me step for step.

It suddenly occurred to me as if I had been struck by a sudden bright light of knowledge. The question popped into my mind, "Where are you going?" Would I simply run until my mother or I collapsed? Would I try to latch onto a passing greyhound? One thing was for sure, if I was not planning to run to Switzerland, I might as well give it up. The farther I ran, the madder my mother got. The madder my mother got, the faster she ran. It was a losing proposition.

It was clear that if my mother caught up with me she would most likely beat me all the way back home. So, the least I could do was try to cut back on some of the mileage. However, as I pondered my fate, I lost track of the fact that I was thinking too fast and running too slow. In what seemed like an eagle swooping down, claws exposed, seeking his prey, my mother's hand grabbed me from behind and yanked my arm, pulling me to a complete stop. I think she yanked me so hard that for a few moments I was back into the previous week.

To say the least she was angry. Not only had I forced her to run after me, but I did it on the busiest roadway in Crisfield. God and country all rubbernecking to see why this woman was chasing a five-year-old young'un with a face full of Band-Aids™. But, in today's world that would have been seen within minutes on YouTube and involved four police cruiser and child services. However, back in the 1960s, it was seen as part of the culture. The young'uns acted like heathens and you chased them down and made sure they had good reason to change their attitude.

I did learn one thing as I had pondered my fate in the brief time I had as my mother grabbed me like a gorilla grabbing a banana. I was right about one thing and wrong about another. I was right when I prophesized that my mother would beat me all the way back home, because she did. However, I was wrong when I thought it would stop once we got there. I cannot recall ever using a Band-Aid™ for anything except a cut since then. But, I can say I am probably the only person in the world who used a Band-Aid™ to create a hurt instead of treating it.

When was I actually 'half-dead?'

My arm was stretched so tight you could have cracked a tick on my elbow. It was not enough to simply raise my hand. It was necessary to hold the extended arm up with the other hand and wave vigorously in order to assure I got Miss McCready's attention.

Miss McCready was deciding who would take the attendance sheet and lunch money down to the school office. You would have thought she was handing out $100 bills. My classmates and I could have beaten a path through an Amazonian jungle with the energy we put behind this multitude of raised hands.

There was something exciting about being the one chosen do something as prestigious as being the "money carrier." Perhaps this is what others thought, but for me it was just the opportunity to get out of class. I would have toted a bucket of snot around my neck if I were sure it would get me out of class.

Man, what a work ethic! I volunteered for every chore. I beat erasers, washed the blackboard, opened and closed classroom windows and Venetian blinds, and was at the ready anytime the teacher needed a message carried to the principal's office.

Of course when there were no chores to be done I had be creative about how I got out of class. I would get thirsty, have the hiccups, develop a weak bladder, or have a sudden case of dry heaves, whatever it took to allow me to escape the walls of the classroom.

All of this creative energy expended for no positive gain. Poor Mom and Dad, here I was volunteering in school for any menial task and at home my parents were lucky to get me do anything outside of breathing. The simplest request was met with endless whining and procrastination.

I can recall my mother asking that I change my clothes when I got home from school before going outside to play. This was certainly an understandable request and one that lacked a great deal of effort. Yea, right, the Berlin wall came down faster than it took me to change my clothes. It was pure attitude. I'm sure that as a child I was not asked to do much that required a great deal of toil. The one task that Dad expected from his teenage son was to feed and water the chickens and ducks before I went to school and after coming home.

I think the year I was in the eighth grade Dad lost three chickens to starvation and a dozen ducks to dehydration. I was simply not dependable. Many were the mornings Dad would greet me with a question about whether I had fed and watered the animals. Having said "No," I would then have to hear Dad's stock reply, "Have you eaten this morning? Then get out there and feed up."

It seemed the only way to get me moving was to threaten bodily harm. With my parents this came in a most harsh manner. They never threaten to kill me. But, I certainly heard that they were going to "beat me half to death" more than once. It seems so much more ruthless to be told you are going to be "half killed."

I always wondered at what point during the beating my parents would conclude that I was actually "half dead." It was too scary too ponder, so I just went ahead and did what I was told in order to avoid having the answer delivered firsthand. I always wondered why I never just did what I was told and got it over with. There were few chores asked of me that would have taken more than 20 minutes to accomplish. Instead, I was 20 minutes trying to get out the duty, and another 20 minutes nursing wounds that came as a result my defiance. Now, I ask you, is this any way to run a childhood?

Getting your face 'busted'

In retrospect, life as a school boy was not as difficult as I once thought. However, there were real issues about my life as a student that had to be dealt with and when you put them in perspective they had their degree of significance. I mean everything is relative. I can certainly look back on my past and trivialize events, however, I have to try and view them as I did as a young boy.

For instance, there was Greg Hanson. Greg was the epitome of hard core, bully material. He was kind of short, but he carried a huge attitude and had no problem expressing his dissatisfaction with school and rules. He also had no problem letting most of us boys know that he would be more than happy to "bust our face." What a horrible thought. Can you imagine how we must have felt about the prospect of having our face busted?

But, where Greg lacked higher morals, he made up in keeping his word. Yes, Greg was a man of his word. I know this because I experienced a very graphic example of it.

It was one day during the fall of 1967. I was in the 5th grade. I was out on the playground at Elementary School # 1, where I attended school from first through sixth grades. There was a special recreational event that I participated in, which involved pretty much every boy in the fourth through sixth grades. It was a simple concept. Two sixth grade boys, I believe it was Jesse Brittingham and Charles Lankford, chose up teams made up of all the other boys in the three grade levels. Each of these two teams became individual "armies" of sorts.

We met out in the far back field behind the school during recess and lunch. What seemed to be hundreds of guys filled the field. One group would march off to the far end of the field and stand grouped in a line. The other would stay at the front of the field in the same pattern. I can still see Jesse raise his hand high in the air and shout "charge!"

At that moment we all took off running toward one another, screaming like wounded banshees. We came together in the middle of the field and pounced on each other like a herd of bi-polar apes, flinging bodies around like Frisbees. It was war! There were random acts of "pile on," of which I almost always lay crumpled up like yesterday's newspaper at the bottom of the pile, my face pushed so far into the grass and dirt that I think I saw a rice field in south China. This went on until either Jesse or Charles decided it was over, or the school bell rang, whichever came first.

On this one day of war, I found myself pushing charging bodies out of my way and tackling several fellows as I tried desperately to stay alive. Unfortunately one of the bodies that I thoughtlessly threw out of my way and onto the waiting ground was that of Greg Hanson. He came up faster than he went down and immediately assumed a boxing stance. Fortunately, the school bell rang and we had to go back to class. I say fortunately, but in reality that was just a temporary stay of execution.

His last words to me were "I will bust your face. "At the end of the school day I began my traditional walk home along Somerset Avenue. Just as I approached the intersection of Chesapeake Avenue, from out of literally nowhere, Greg stepped out from behind a bush. He looked at me with eyes as cold as steel, as he forced on a pair of black, leather gloves. He looked at me and in a second's time he punched me square in the mouth. It was quick, but forceful. It happened so fast, I was shocked and temporarily left disoriented. By the time I came to my senses, blood was flowing out of my lip and Greg was gone. Dazed, I stumbled down the street, realizing that if I could say little pleasant about Greg Hanson, I had to admit he was a man of his word. He did what he said he would do, he busted by face.

Now, just for the record, Greg's last name is not Hanson. However, he is still alive, and the last time I talked to someone in Crisfield, he still had at least two fists. So, I will be happy to not tempt fate and simply rely on my memory in terms of my experience of having my face busted.

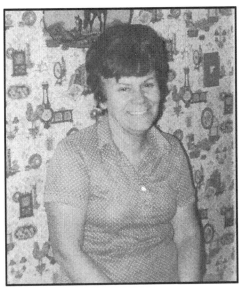

She may look docile in this photo, but trust me,
lock her out of the house at 20 below zero,
and it's a different story.

Hell hath no fury like Mom freezing

If I live to be a thousand I will never forget the day I awoke to a grotesque, blood-red, raging face, hovering only inches from me. Though at first glance it appeared to be a demon or some other horrific monster, I learned within seconds that it was in fact, my mother.

I recall as a young boy there were a couple of unwritten rules that I used to guide me through daily life in my household. Number one, avoid making Mom mad when she was holding a cooking utensil and number two, avoid making Dad mad...period.

As I have often written in my columns, it was never a mystery about how Dad would react to heathen actions from his children. He spoke loudly and carried a belt. We knew Dad's style left no room for error on our part. Though he was strict, we could always count on Dad being consistent and he was fair. I can honestly say that I never encountered Dad's wrath without it being deserved.

Mom was less predictable. She left the lion's share of the discipline issues up to Dad. The only thing we could really count on as being truly predictable in Mom's case whenever we were acting like wild boars, was hearing her say several times a day, "Just wait, HE will be home soon." This may sound minor; however, to us it was as if she was talking about God. All I could envision was Dad barreling through the front door with a belt in each hand.

But, occasionally Mom would actually dole out the discipline. However in her case it had to be spontaneous. It was like watching a pot of water boil. She would put up with us acting like hyenas for a short while and then once hitting the breaking point, she would strike. The problem for us young'uns was we never knew what activity she may be undertaking when she finally reached her breaking point.

If she was combing her hair we would get struck with a long, black, hard-plastic comb. If she was getting dressed we could expect a shoe or slipper to fly by, hopefully missing tender parts.

However, this one day it was not so much a fear of what utensil Mom may have at her ready; but more the simple rage that blanketed her face. As a teenager I would sometimes spend Saturday mornings in and out of bed, often sleeping until noon.

It was a winter morning, especially cold, and a bitter, cutting wind drove the temperatures even further past the freezing mark. I got up out of bed long enough to eat a Pop-Tart™ and notice that Mom was not home. At the time I was the only soul in the house. Feeling the urge to gain a few more precious moments in my warm bed upstairs, I finished off my Pop-Tart™ and headed back upstairs.

However, before making the trek, I did something that carried neither rhyme nor reason, and proved to be a fatal mistake. I suppose out of habit, I locked the back door before heading back to bed. It was customary for the front door to stay pretty much always locked, this because we always used the backdoor as our entrance and exit.

So, off to bed I went. I was not long drifting off into a soothing, much needed sleep. I cannot even guess how long after falling asleep that I was ripped out of my state of slumber like a wrapper from my brother's Fudgesicle™.

It was at that precise moment that I found myself staring into the flaming eyes of what at first appeared to be a demon straight from the dark abyss. But, I was not long recognizing this as none other than Mom. Her face was blood red and her eyes seemed to be literally popping out of their sockets. Her hands were rigid and her fingernails were grabbing at me, attempting to pull me out of the bed by my face. She was screaming at a pitch so high it sounded more like dolphins.

It seems that Mom, who at the time was pregnant with my sister, had gone to the grocery store and when arriving home found herself standing at a locked backdoor. This after she climbed the tall, steep back steps with multiple bags of groceries in her arms, battling the below freezing temperatures and the artic winds. She apparently beat on the door and hollered trying to get my attention, but my radio and deep sleep kept me from responding. To this day I cannot recall how she actually was able to make entrance into the house. But, it would not have surprised me if she had torn through the kitchen and up the steps to my bedroom without even opening a door.

I do think, however, that after that wintry morning I gained a whole new respect for my mother.

Just put a sweater on, or take it off

Man, I can't believe this is happening to me! How many times have you heard yourself say that? Well, this past week I found myself saying it quite a lot. It all started when the weather took a turn for the cool side. I am running low on fuel oil, so I turn the heat on just enough to take the chill off the house.

I was on my way to work and knew my son would be getting up soon, so I left the heat on at a bare minimum so he would be comfortable as he got ready for work himself. I went to work at about 5 a.m., so at about 7:45 a.m., I called home to remind my son to turn the heat off when he left for work at 8 a.m. He assured me he would and I relaxed realizing I was doing the best I could to conserve fuel for the bitter winter ahead.

At about 4:30 p.m., my son called me at work. He had gotten home and realized something was seriously wrong. "Dad, please don't get mad. I have done something really stupid," he said to me. I knew then that my world as I knew it, was about to end. He then told me that instead of turning the heat off when he left at 8 a.m., he turned the knob the wrong way and left the heat at full blast for the entire day.

"My God, I can't believe this is happening to me," I thought to myself. I scrimp and scrape, trying to save a nickel and my son has turned my house into a blast furnace. Just throw dirt all me, I'm dead. Why? Why? I literally began to weep. In my mind the entire time I see my house surrounded with heat ripples and dollar bills rolling out the windows. What could be worse? I had to ask. Two hours later my son calls from his workplace. He was called back into work and forgot to turn the air conditioner off of the house. What air-conditioner? Why would you have the air conditioner on? Of course, how silly of me, you were hot because you left the heat on 2000-degrees all day. So, you turn the air-conditioner on to cool down the house and now it's blowing $50 bills out of the air vents. Why do I even try? How can I ever get ahead?

Suddenly, I recall my youth and how my father felt about these things. I remember my father coming home in the winter finding one of us had left the back door slightly ajar. "Are we heating all outdoors," he would scream as he slammed the door shut. I could not understand why Dad felt this way about the door being left open. Now I do.

I can still see Dad shoving comic books and pages of the daily newspaper into the cracks around the front door. An entire year's subscription to the Daily Times would be hanging around the front door frame. Yes, I thought my dad was a tightwad. Now, I find myself saying the same words that my father used to say all winter long. "It ain't cold in here. There ain't any need to turn the heat up. Go put on a sweater."

Halloween was a major event

I can't believe the obnoxious behavior of whoever was responsible for the vandalism in the area last week. Spray painting cars and houses in the dark of the night is without a doubt the work of cowardice morons with no respect for other people's property. I have certainly lacked respect in my lifetime and have probably been involved in a variety of incidents that I should not have been involved in, but to destroy someone else's hard-earned property is outrageous.

I guess times have changed, but I can't recall such destructive actions during Halloween when I was growing up. And, believe me, if anyone was capable of wreaking havoc in widespread ignorant behavior it was a bunch of Crisfield young'uns. The only thing we really feared on Halloween was that someone would turn over our outhouse. As important as the outhouse was to family life I can't imagine why people didn't put a brick foundation under it and moor it to concrete posts. No, the outhouse only needed a couple of good-sized boys to tip it over. So, you see, it was easy prey on Halloween.

I think I went all week not going to the outhouse fearing that hoodlums would come early and dump the toilet while I was inside. I'm serious. You can't figure out a hoodlum's schedule. I mean he could come on the night that you expect, or he could throw everything off and come a night early, or even a night later. It's all in the delivery. The more surprised and off guard the outhouse owner is, the more fun the hoodlum has. Only in Crisfield these people were not called hoodlums. They were called heathens, punks or rednecks.

I guess I just remember Halloween as the night Mom took us out Trick-or-Treating. There were three of us boys and Mom and Dad did not go all out for Halloween. Mom figured if we all had a mask we were set. Mom's friend Pat Diggs would bring her kids to our house to meet for the Halloween run. All seven of us would pile into Pat's Pontiac and head out. We did about 99 percent of our Halloween trick-or-treating on Hall Street and Wyndfall Avenue, where Mom said the rich people lived.

Mom and Pat would drop us off and drive off and wait for us what seemed to be a mile and half up the road. Now, I never realized it then, but now I know that to Mom and Pat we were nothing more than mules, pack horses, and hay haulers. It was our job to go door-to-door and load up on candy; candy that was for all intent purposes our candy. However, when we got home Mom would have us dump our bags and she would methodically pick and choose her favorites. I guess I didn't mind, because I was too busy digging through the bag looking for money to know what she was doing.

All in all, I guess I didn't mind trick-or-treating, except that I always dreamed of having a full costume. We would go door-to-door and usually there would be a group of trick-or-treaters who would be gathered in front a home. It seemed to be common courtesy to wait until there was a mob gathered before knocking on the door. There would be a pirate, Superman, Batman, a Princess, a clown, all in full regalia. Then there was me, wearing a plastic devil's mask and a flannel shirt and overalls.

One year my Dad got into the act and came home after having apparently found a deal at a local gas station where you got a free Halloween mask for every 10 gallons of gas. Here he stood in the doorway with two of the ugliest masks

I have ever seen. I don't mean they were scary, I mean they were just plain ugly. One was a dog mask and the other was a wolf mask. These were the types of mask that fit over the face with a rubber band and had a nose that stuck out about 12 inches to give a three-dimensional effect. The real kicker was the ears. To add a flavor of reality, the mask maker had attached 10-inch, black felt ears that dangled from the head. I was not excited about the prospects of wearing this hideous plastic monstrosity but also not at all excited about challenging Dad's sudden burst of generosity.

So, off we went to terrorize Crisfield residents with our dog and wolf masks. The nose on the dog mask stuck so far off from my mask that the people struck me in the face when they opened the door. I think I forgot more candy because they felt sorry for me.

I remember walking down the street hoping to get from house to house without being recognized by any of my classmates. I know Dad meant well, but I began to wonder if there was an ulterior motive to his madness with these masks. As I headed down the road wind blew the ears in front of my eyes. There I was stumbling down the street, eyes covered by my ears and desperately trying to carry my bag of goodies without tripping.

It was "Trick-or-Treat from hell." By the time I got ready to go back home I had torn the ears off the mask and the nose looked like an accordion. It was such a bad experience that the next year I did trick-or-treat dressed as a woman. That's an entirely different story altogether.

Facing mortality while up a tree

At the age of 12, I could run from the front steps of my family home on Richardson Avenue in Crisfield, to the front door of Archie Tyler's store across the street without taking a second breath. Today, it seems I can't walk from the living room couch to the bathroom without stopping to take a nap. I remember as a young boy I could climb trees like a spider monkey. My friends and I would climb trees and swing from branch to branch, all the while shooting at one another with tree branch rifles. Tarzan had nothing on me.

It was in the early 1980s when my son, who at the time was about eight years old, and I were in the front yard flying a balsa wood airplane. The plane was doing real well until high winds carried it into a huge tree that sits in my front yard. My son became very distressed that his plane was now perched high up in the branches of the tree. You could see the tail of the plane protruding from a clump of branches near the very top.

I assured my son that I would quickly retrieve the plane and bring it back to him for future flights. I saw that the branches just below the lodged plane were very thick and would certainly hold up under my weight. Off I went.

Immediately my mind was cast back a dozen years. The familiar feel of bark under my fingers was a welcome shot to my male ego. I zipped up the tree like there was a pile of $100 bills waiting for me at the top. Before I knew it I was just inches away from the plane. Bear in mind that during my trip up the tree I had been so focused on getting to the top without breaking a limb (both on the tree and on my own body) that I did not pay attention to the sights around me.

As I grabbed for the plane I looked down at my son. He looked about the size of a chunk of coal. It was at that moment that I realized I was what seemed like at the time, 1,000 feet off the ground. All of a sudden, I know longer cared to be in touch with my inner child or my male ego. I wanted to be in touch with the ground. I literally froze. I could not find the courage to move my foot from the branch it was perched on to the branch below. I was now faced with the prospect of building a tree house and having all my possessions transported up the tree with me, because I was too scared to come down.

I thought I was facing the worst part of this episode when I realized I had to tell my young son that I was afraid to begin my climb down the tree. My concern was that he would simply tell me to throw down his plane and I could live up in the tree like a bald eagle. My son always looked up to me; now he was really looking up to me, about 25-feet up to be exact. Just when I thought things had gotten about as bad as they could get, my wife stepped out the front door.

She saw our son staring up at the top of the tree and became curious when she did not see me. She came out into the front yard and when she saw me in the tree, she informed me that dinner was ready. It was then my humiliating duty to inform her that I was up in the tree and couldn't get down; so much for my male ego.

If I had told my wife that we had just won the $28 million lottery, she could not have been more excited than she was that I was stuck up in that tree. Her first words were, "Hey, I better call the fire department." Then she headed for the house.

All of a sudden I envisioned this huge red ladder truck pulling up to our house, followed by a newspaper reporter and a television news crew. This gave me the incentive to attempt to move my legs and feet. I begged my wife, and I mean begged, to not call the fire department, but instead pull our Dodge station wagon up under the tree.

As I nervously made my way from branch to branch, it was the taunting of my wife, who kept insisting she would call the fire department, the police, the city public works department, the dog catcher, the undertaker, anybody who would be able to witness this once in a lifetime spectacle and make sure it was broadcast to the rest of the city.

Finally my feet were able to rest on the top of the car. It was a quick jump down to the ground. As I walked toward my son his first words were, "Daddy, my plane is still in the tree." Yes, in my scared-stiff state, I had forgotten to bring the plane back down with me. But, as luck would have it, a gust of wind blew the plane free and it floated to the ground; in my estimation, about 20 minutes too late.

This cartoon, drawn by local pastor and artist, Karen Bongard,
ran with this column in the December 1997 issue of the
Seaford and Laurel Star newspapers.

11th hour Christmas shopping

I love the Christmas season, but it amazes me how much
of a contrast exists between the spirit of the season and the
reality of an hour spent Christmas shopping. For the first
time in at least a dozen years, I decided to start my
Christmas shopping before December 23. I was looking
forward to avoiding the last-minute rush, because after all,
everybody knows that by starting early you will not have to

face the horrendous crowd of eleventh-hour maniacs. Wrong.

It appears that starting early means starting in June. I went into the stores at the beginning of December and found nothing different from those times that I had waited until Christmas Eve. No one believes it when I say that I actually made it a practice for many years to do Christmas shopping on Christmas Eve. It wasn't planned that way, I am a procrastinator, and a broke procrastinator at that. It would easily be December 21, before I would give serious thought to Christmas shopping.

At the time when I was married, my wife made sure that we had all the Christmas shopping for our son and the rest of our family and friends finished by early December. That just left us to shop for one another. I recall one year that after leaving a Christmas party, my former wife went to bed and I realized I had not finished buying her presents. So, I did what any faithful husband would do. It was 2 a.m. and there I was, standing in the aisle of the local Shore Stop™ convenience store.

As I walked down the aisles I studied each and every item that was stocked on the shelves. I had to find that special something that would light up my wife's eyes on Christmas morning. I became frantic. The closest I came to finding something to light up her eyes was a four-pack of 100-watt light bulbs. This didn't look good. Extension cords, 30 amp fuses, and assorted boxes of breakfast cereals. Dear Lord, what will I do?

I looked outside and I could actually see the sun coming up. Only a few hours and my then eight-year-old son would be bounding out of bed and rapping on our bedroom door, demanding to see what Santa had brought.

I searched each and every aisle and just as I finished reading the title of all the major washing detergents, I saw them. They hung from the hook, seemingly shining in the stores florescent lighting. "I'm saved," I thought to myself. I went over to the wall and carefully lifted the last pair of brown, cotton, industrial work gloves off of a metal hook. "Wouldn't these look wonderful on my wife's hands," I thought to myself. "They're perfect. What 28-year-old woman would not want a pair of brown, cotton, industrial work gloves?"

I suddenly had a reality check; my wife. That's what woman would not want a pair of brown, cotton, industrial work gloves. I envision my wife's face as she opened the box and pulled out the gloves. It would be worse than the time I gave her a vacuum cleaner and frying pan for her birthday. Yes, I used to believe that every woman wanted some type of cooking or cleaning utensil for those special holiday gifts.

I went home a defeated man that Christmas Eve, 10 years ago. I found nothing that would make the grade. So, I gave her a card with some well-meaning verse and a promise of a candlelight dinner, or some such romantic malarkey. I don't know if this Christmas debacle anything to do with it, but this woman and I are no longer married.

Well, I no longer wait to do last-minute Christmas shopping, but I still find it frustrating that the emphasis on this special holiday is on buying presents. It seems we wind up measuring the value of our relationships, whether family or friends, by what type of gift we can buy.

I guess things have gotten to the point of no return in terms of a commercialized Christmas, but hopefully somewhere in all the hustle and bustle, we will take a moment and reflect on why we celebrate this holiday.

If, when we pass by a nativity scene that is displayed in someone's yard or business, we are able to understand that this is the reason for the Christmas season, then I suppose all is not lost.

Memories: Movies of our past

They seem much like dreams now, and memories of my childhood can sometimes be vivid and at other times somewhat sketchy. I suppose not being physically connected to our past enables us to oftentimes see those days of old as seemingly more free of emotion, both good and bad. It is much like watching a movie that plays in our head.

So, how hot was the summer and how cold was the winter? I suppose we rely on our memories to simply express what we remember. There is no doubt that we had very cold winters when I was growing up; how else would I recall the snot freezing to my upper lip? And likewise, summer must have produced some very hot days, because I can recall stepping in the hot, black road tar that had melted beneath my bare feet. I can also remember looking down Richardson Avenue for the full distance down to the docks and actually seeing the heat rise from the asphalt.

Someone stopped me in a restaurant the other day and asked me how I was able to recall the events of my youth so clearly. I felt she may have been hinting that I make some of these events up. I assured her that if I were to be making anything up, I would certainly make myself appear a little less full of heathenism. I have reached the conclusion that most of us who were born pre-1980 had somewhat similar childhoods, just occurring in different places and different times. I am sure like me; they are able to recall their childhood as easily as I do. Some situations; however, are much more clear than others.

I can recall at seven or eight years of age sitting in Ira Lowe's barber chair, getting my customary "crew cut" hairdo. I can still see the barbershop as Ira Lowe would turn me around in the barber chair. I recall looking outside of the window that faced the street. Ira Lowe's barbershop was located on Fourth Street, just off Main Street. This was considered to be the "black side of town." Sadly, the divisions in the community were nothing anyone gave a second thought about. I just recall as I looked out the window of the barber shop I never saw, nor did I expect to see, a white face among those who passed by.

As I would turn and face the various angles of the room, I could see lined up on the counter top the various electric shearing tools that he used to trim up our hair. The scissors were inside a large glass container filled with what appeared to be a blue liquid, I assume for sterilization. Hanging on the back wall was the small vacuum cleaner that Ira Lowe would use to suck the loose hair off the back of our shirts. Next to this was a long, leather razor strap. I can still almost hear him slap the sharp, shiny razor up and down the strap before he would run the razor across the back of our neck to give us a smooth cut. Later, Ira Lowe would use the razor to cut the dead ends off the top of my hair when I was allowed to grow my hair a bit longer than the traditional crew cut.

Also hanging on the wall of the barbershop was a special seat that Ira Lowe would put in the barber chair when children would come in and need to be raised higher than the barber chair would allow. I suppose it would be considered a booster chair by today's standards. I remember how elated my brothers and I were when we were finally considered old enough to no longer need the booster seat. At the end of each haircut, Ira Lowe would hand us a shiny dime. It was such a tradition that this became the main reason we would be excited to get our haircut. That tiny piece of silver would, as Dad would say, "burn a hole" in my pocket until I could get somewhere to spend it.

Ira Lowe spoke few words to us as he cut our hair. He would more often trade conversation with the old men who sat in the five or six, iron chairs that lined the front wall, reading comic books and newspapers. Smoke filled the room from their cigarettes, cigars and pipes.

Though he spoke few words to us, Ira Lowe still remains a central character in the memories of my childhood. He ranks up there with Archie Tyler, Ruby Dize, Miss Addie Justice, Webb White and "Skagg." I recall the last conversation I had with Ira Lowe, which closed out that era of my life. It was in the year of 1972. I had finally reached a point when Dad gave up the fight to keep me from growing my hair long. I let my hair grow without having it cut and then walked in Ira Lowe's barbershop. He looked at me and said, "I don't do long haircuts. You will have to find a barber who can do that type of haircut for a man." I turned and walked out of the barbershop, leaving the first of what would be many remnants of my youth behind.

A simple, but scary Christmas

I miss the simple, old-fashioned Christmases of my youth; the Christmases spent with my grandmother, mother and father and brothers. Okay, forget the bull. I miss the Christmases where my parents did all the buying and I did all the getting. But, it really does seem that things were a little more simplistic back then. I guess my mother and father may disagree, but it seems that way to me.

For one thing, the varieties of presents that children have to pick from are of a massive volume. As a child I would become spastic when the new Sears and Roebuck Wish Book catalog came in the mail. By the time my brothers and I were done tearing into it to see the latest toys available, there was nothing left between the covers of the book except kitchenware and ladies lingerie. I can still see the toys that would be shown in all their glorious color inside that Wish Book. Each turn of the page created a new desire; a new idea of what I wanted that year. For me, it was the pearl handled western guns and accompanying holster set. I loved to watch "The Wild, Wild West" television show and fancied myself another James West. My brother was more intelligent than me. He enjoyed microscopes, telescopes and chemistry sets. His fingers are just now healing from the concoction he brewed at age 11, made from a strange mix of chemicals that caused the skin to peel off of all 10 of his fingers. It amazes me now, that even though I know times were tough for my parents back then with three young boys, they always seemed to manage that we got that one special gift we were longing for.

So, each Christmas morning we would stand side-by-side to have a picture taken. I with my pearl handle sidearm, my older brother displaying his briefcase filled with test tubes and chemicals, and my younger brother garnishing a sophisticated "Man from U.N.C.L.E." secret agent's gun. What a Kodak moment. Wait a minute. This sounds more like a toddler terrorist group. You would think our parents were the head of a future militia group. My God, we could have been featured on an episode of "Hard Copy," or on the cover of "Soldier of Fortune" magazine.

But, really, these were not the only gifts we received. My older brother, being the studious, intellectual type, always received a plethora of mystery and science fiction books. My younger brother would always get some type of racing car set, or "Matchbox™" cars. Me? Well, it was customary each year that I get - "Cooties."

That's right. Year after year, my parents would make sure I had the latest edition of the "Cootie Bug™" game. I had the original Cooties, the new and improved Cooties and advanced stages of Cooties. I think they still sell these creatures, but I never got them for my own son because I feared there may be some stigma attached to the receiving of a gift like this. I mean its bed lice in a box, for Heaven's sake. All those years were my parents trying to tell me something? I mean, the object of the game was to build a big cootie bug. I can't think of any other gift that you would give that could match the negative perception of this game, unless you gift wrapped a "Roach Motel."

Man, things have sure changed. Now the gift lists include the 64-bit Nintendo™, "Tickle Me Elmo" and "Holiday Barbie;" and that's just for the adults. Kids are getting home computers and video cameras. It's no wonder that my son looks at me like I have two heads when I tell him how neat the View Master was to get as a gift. I was in seventh heaven when I saw my first "Give-a -show Projector." Yes, things have changed since I was a kid. But, I guess that's what it's all about change, progress, a continual development into state of the art technology.

But, make no mistake about it. I may live with change to a degree, but, we must be careful. After all, what kind of Christmas would it be if we didn't get to see Santa Claus sliding down the hill on an electric razor?

Here are the three terrors with our mother. That is Mom, towering over her three hoodlums. Then there are (left to right) my younger brother, Jeff, me, and my older brother Tommy. Looming behind us is our beautiful, shapeless Christmas tree.

Dusting with a buzzard wing

The recent cold wave has me longing for summer. Not only has it been cold, but the wind has made outside my house more like the Yukon. Like most fickle people, I will complain about the cold and long for the heat of summer only to adjust my complaining when summer arrives and start moaning about the extreme heat.

But, for some reason, summer brings back more memories of my carefree days of youth. I can remember the days when me and my brothers ran around the yards near my home clothed in nothing more than a pair of stretch waist short pants; no shirt, no shoes, no pride. We would charge outside in the summertime no later than 8 a.m. By noon we looked like refugees from the Amazon jungle. Sweaty dirt beads clinging to our necks like 12 inches of hair. We would start the day off with a pair of rubber, 10-Cent Store flip-flops and by 10 a.m. our feet would be so dirty that it looked like we were wearing socks. The flip-flops would have been run so roughshod through the neighborhood that they would be reduced to nothing more than one flip and a flop. The plastic strap that was positioned between our toes would have long been ripped out through the base of the sandal and the destroyed shoe would be lying in some bushes near our house.

Yes, those summers in Crisfield were hot. I remember looking down Richardson Avenue toward the A&P Store and the old Seafood Laboratory and watching the heat waves rising up from the concrete. I well remember stepping in the melted tar that was put down between sections of the roadway and sidewalks. The tar would melt from the heat and then stick to our feet and toes like hot glue. The blacktop parking lots were as hot as the surface of the sun and we looked like peg-legged young'uns running to the front doors of the store.

My mother and grandmother would sit on the front porch and hold prayer vigils asking Jesus for a breeze; all the while waving Bradshaw & Sons Funeral Home paper fans on a stick in front of their faces to try and stay cool.

I think the only difference in hot weather when I was a child and the summers we experience today, is less the weather itself and more our lack of tolerance for it. We had no air conditioned homes or cars when I was a child. Most of the stores in Crisfield had huge ceiling fans that kept the air moving, but no central air conditioning.

We went to bed, woke up and lived out the day in whatever temperature came with the day. Our ability to deal with the heat had to have been much better because we knew of nothing better, outside of taking turns sticking our heads in the Frigidaire. Today we have air conditioning everywhere we go. We are able to sleep in it, drive in it and shop in it. So, I think we are now spoiled and when the heat rises above 80 degrees and humidity creeps up, we are less able to deal with it.

I remember going to my grandmother's house and there were nothing more than the windows being open to deal with the summer air. She would be sitting at the kitchen table fanning her face with yesterday's paper and the wood cooking stove running hot enough to melt metal.

I was always impressed with how frugal my grandparent's lived their daily lives. They grew their own food, whether sprouting from the ground or flying or walking on four legs. I remember vividly seeing my grandmother dusting her furniture with the severed wing of a Turkey Buzzard. Now, that is frugal, or perhaps simply morbid.

But, I miss those old days, even though they represented simple moments, void of the fast-paced daily existence of today's world. We had no technology, no trendy clothes, and few were the times we had actual spending money. Perhaps we were lacking, but thankfully it never occurred to me at the time.

My kitchen sink is like a landfill

Having been a bachelor for the past 12 years, I have learned to fully appreciate all the duties that my mother performed around the house when I was a child. I can remember my mother standing at the kitchen sink, soap suds rolling down her arms, dish rag in her hand, washing the day's dirty dishes.

No matter how big the pile of dishes was in the sink, I can still recall that rather than washing a glass out, I would reach in the cupboard and get a clean glass for water. I would then add that glass to the dirty dish pile. Now, as I approach what I admit is more than a day's worth of dirty dishes, I can understand how even the small job of washing dishes can be a monumental undertaking at the end of a workday.

My mother had a habit of warning me and my brothers that one day we would have kids and she hoped they would "dirty up as many dishes as you all do." Well, Mom's prophecy came truer than true. Not only did I have a child, but he turned out to be a "master of mess;" not only in the kitchen, but throughout the house. I have a tendency to procrastinate. If I see the dishes or laundry piling up, I tend to turn my head and act as if I don't see it. By the time I get around to addressing the problem the dishes are piled in the sink up to the water spigots and cover every inch of counter space in the room.

I have to begin making room on the counter so that I can get the dishes out of the sink to begin running my dishwater. As I pull out cereal bowls with week-old Fruit Loops caked to the sides and bottom, the stench of equally old milk causes me to gag. I am given a quick rundown of the foods that my son and I have eaten that week; as a good part of it is lying at the bottom of the sink.

My son seems to have an aversion to emptying his plate before shoving it into the sink to join the other breakfast, lunch and dinner artifacts. I found soggy toast, half eaten tacos, pizza crust and spaghetti noodles floating in my dishwater. This of course joins the lumps of coagulated milk that has settled in the sink strainer. I know this does not paint a very pretty picture. Believe me, this is not a pretty picture. The most frightening part of it all is that this food was once something we were eating.

I cannot understand why I will not gather the wherewithal it takes to combat the dishes before they become so out of control. I've even gone out and bought dishes to keep from facing the pit of crud-covered eating utensils that awaits me in the kitchen. I realize it is petty laziness that keeps me from keeping abreast of the dirty dish situation, but believe me, I pay for it once I get started on the task.

It has gotten so bad that at times I have had to use a screwdriver and a pair of pliers to separate the glasses from the plates. I once had some type of food product welded so tightly to the outside of the bowls and glasses that rather than resort to a hammer and chisel, I simply threw them in the trash and bought new dishes. Laundry is no different. Last week I knew I had waited too long to do the laundry because when I went into the bedroom, I couldn't find my king-sized bed; there were clothes everywhere.

My son makes an athletic event out of taking his dirty clothes to the laundry basket. The clothes basket is in my bedroom; so on the way from his bed into the shower, he opens my door at shoots three-pointers at the clothes basket. Usually he misses the basket and I have socks hanging on my dresser mirror and wet bath towels hanging on the headboard of my bed like funeral drapes.

With New Year's approaching perhaps I will make a resolution to try addressing dishes and laundry on a daily basis. Well, maybe not daily, but certainly twice a week. Or, what's wrong with weekly? All I know is the visions in my mind of my mother standing at the sink with perspiration dotting her forehead, or her carrying loads of laundry to the Laundromat make me realize Mom was a saint.

Welcome to my summer nightmare

I was talking to my good friend, retired Delaware State Trooper Ray Callaway, the other day. Ironically, Ray like me, has history in my native Crisfield, Md. He has family in Crisfield and spent time there as a young boy. Recently Ray and his wife purchased a place in Crisfield near one of my favorite hangouts, "Brick Hill."

Ray and I were reminiscing about time spent on the beach at Brick Hill, which is located on the grounds of the Crisfield American Legion. I haven't visited that part of town for a few decades and Ray encouraged me to drive down and see how much it has changed and developed. Apparently a great many people from out of the area have discovered the natural beauty of Crisfield, especially along the waterfront.

Mom would tote us down to Brick Hill in an attempt to burn off some of her young'uns boundless energies. Brick Hill was close, cheap and a better option than beating us half to death as we had a tendency to push our energy in the wrong direction. I remember my Mom's best friend, Pat Diggs, and her husband Hayes, operated a concession stand at Brick Hill, so we could get lunch while we were there.

I suppose Brick Hill was one of the places that we first learned to swim. It was a salt water experience that was riddled with crabs and sea nettles. Sea nettles had a knack for ruining what was a really enjoyable day of swimming. These creatures would come in with the tide and quickly turn our fun into misery.

We would be frolicking around in the water like a bunch of sea monkeys and all of a sudden there would be sharp pain on our legs and arms. We knew the sea nettles were moving in. Like a dish of floating jelly dragging a mass of stringy tentacles, these beasts would not so much attack, but more simply pass by. As they would pass by their slippery tentacles would slide across our skin like slimy branding irons.

We would always try to hang in for as long as we could, but once the tide started coming in more aggressively, so would the sea nettles. Eventually, one by one we would succumb to the invasion and get out of the water. I think this is why I liked the beach at Ocean City; there were no sea nettles. The water was far too rough for them, but not rough enough for us heathen boneheads.

There was a difference between sea nettles and Jelly Fish. Jelly Fish were gorgeous, transparent works of art that would glide through the water like a portable Picasso. Unlike their ugly step-siblings, the Jelly Fish did not reach out and sting you. It would simply float by like a water-logged summer cloud. You almost wanted to wave as it passed by; such gentle souls. However, I do recall one time that I was unintentionally stung by a large Jelly Fish; well unintentional as far as the Jelly Fish was concerned.

My buddy Hayes "Satch" Diggs and I were playing along the beach at Brick Hill as the tide was going out. Sometimes these jelly creatures would be left behind on the sand as the water regressed. This one particular Jelly Fish was rather large; about the size of a dinner plate. Satch picked it up as it was customary to help them back into the fleeing waters. He called me over and asked me to look at the design on the Jelly Fish's back. I should have recognized this as a ploy. As I approached he thrust the Jelly Fish into my face. It literally covered my entire face and head, which is quite a statement toward the size of this Jelly Fish. I can still to this very day see the view I had from within the Jelly Fish, much like I would imagine the quality of vision with full-blown cataracts. I also recall the extreme burning that immediately consumed both eye sockets. As I have said before, we Crisfield young'uns knew how to have a good time.

In my memories of youth, Crisfield was plagued by sea nettles, mosquitos and horse flies. If you could battle your way through these summer plagues, there was opportunity for a good time. I suppose I may take my friend Ray Callaway's advice and drive down to Brick Hill and see how it has developed. Then again, maybe I won't.

The hazards of the bottom bunk

I will start this column with a warning. For those readers who are squeamish, perhaps you should not read my column today. I will apologize in advance for the graphic nature of this particular article.

I recently spent time at my mother's house having dinner with my family. It is amazing that regardless of what is major in the news headlines, our mealtime conversation will eventually turn to the subject of what it was like as kids growing up in Crisfield.

We recently talked about a subject that was less than appealing during dinner, yet it is a topic that everyone can identify with. I remember it like it was yesterday. Having spent several years sleeping in a three-quarter-size bed with my older brother, my parents were faced with having to make room for the number three son who was quickly outgrowing his crib.

Rather than risk having three hooligans in the bed at one time, Mom and Dad decided they would purchase beds to accommodate us all.

There was a sale at Olsen's Furniture Store in Pocomoke City, and Dad bought a set of bunk beds at a really good price. It was decided that my younger brother, Jeff, would have the three-quarter bed to himself and my older brother and I would occupy the bunk beds. Of course there was the traditional argument about who would get the top bunk.

My brother, Tommy, argued that he was the oldest and should have the pick of the bunks. My parents cited the fact that I was prone to restless sleeping, including often violent nightmares which involved walking in my sleep. They feared that I would be more likely to pitch myself off the top bunk during one of these dream sequences, so my older brother got the top bunk.

I think back and realize that the arrangement my brother and I had was less than cooperative. He would nestle in at night and turn on the radio to KDKA talk radio. I would nestle into the bottom bunk and turn my radio on to WCAO, a Top 40 radio station. All night we would be blaring different radio stations. It sounded more like the center floor of a Wall Street brokerage than a bedroom. Nonetheless, that was the way things were at our house.

This one night that comes to mind started as every bedtime before. I can recall having my face turned toward the wall as I prepared to try and go to sleep. That was the last thing I remember before the incident. I do remember vividly having a dream that someone turned on the water flow to a fire hydrant on Richardson Avenue, outside our house.

I guess during my dream I turned over in my bed and when I opened my eyes I was faced with the most horrifying sight imaginable. My older brother had his head hanging over his top bunk and a literal delicatessen of food was pouring out of his mouth. I was quickly ducking pieces of bologna, potatoes, macaroni noodles and chunks of peanut butter. I can recall that my mother heard my brother getting sick and came into the bedroom to comfort him. However, that comforting came at a cost. She had to clean up the mess.

Watching my mother try to clean up after my brother's sporadic episodes of sickness was much like watching a cat deal with a hairball.

She would take a roll of paper towels, tear off a few sheets and with her head turned away from the mess, stick her toweled hand in the direction of the mess as if she was playing pin the tail on the donkey. As she recklessly moved her hand in and out she would be in a constant state of gagging. It was a pitiful sight.

This would go on until my father would tire of it and eventually take over the job. But, though she wasn't good at cleaning up the messes, my mother was great at consoling us. She would rub our head with a wet, cold cloth and hug us until it felt better. It was great if I was the object of this affection, but when she was consoling one of my siblings, the sight of it almost caused me to get sick.

I think if I'm not mistaken, after that incident with my brother, I slept in a raincoat and riot mask.

My older brother, Tommy (left), and me share a chair a few years before we shared bunk beds.

Who moved my pickle loaf?

Standing on the back porch I could see her coming around the side of her house, she had a towel wrapped around her shoulders and she was sporting blue hair. No, it was not the way the sun hit her freshly bobby pin-clustered hair; she actually had blue hair.

Miss Addie Justice was well into her 80s and cast a high class shadow. Her home was a historic three-story house that was immaculate and adorned with many expensive antiques. On the limited occasions we were allowed to visit in her house, Miss Addie made sure that our path went directly into the foyer of the home and never beyond the dining room.

She had a kitchen, but owned no refrigerator. She kept all her perishables in the refrigerator at our house. So, twice a day this elderly little woman would trudge across the yard and enter our home to retrieve her goods. I recall one day she was unable to find a brand new package of pickled-loaf lunch meat she had left in the refrigerator the day before.

My older brother Tommy, only ate bologna and hated the thought of any meat that would contain bits of pickles and who knows what else. My younger brother Jeff, was not even eating solid food at that point. Because my mother was acutely aware that I absolutely loved pickle loaf lunchmeat; but mainly because I ate like a starving refugee, all eyes fell on me as the culprit who stole Miss Addie's pickled-loaf lunch meat.

So great was the circumstantial evidence against me, that I even started thinking that I possibly stole the pickle loaf in my sleep. I think Mom bought Miss Addie another package of pickle loaf and made great apologies on my behalf. I was considered to be the "greedy little heathen" who could not respect the sanctity of someone else's pickle loaf.

It was a very emotional experience for me realizing that there was no way to prove my innocence. Back in those days there was no such thing as DNA testing. However, just a few days later I received a reprieve when while cleaning and defrosting the refrigerator, Mom pulled out one of the meat trays and down in the lower rear part of the refrigerator was Miss Addie's missing package of pickle loaf. While I may have been vindicated, I do not recall any mass efforts of apology from anyone in my family or Miss Addie for that matter.

Be that as it may, we were ordered by my father to be extra respectful to Miss Addie because she was an older lady. Dad had a passion for respecting older people. He would be well prepared to assure that we maintained that same level of respect, even if he had to beat it into us.

I actually really liked and respected Miss Addie. She would go away each winter to live with one of her daughters in Baltimore. When she came home in the summer, she would always have some type of trinket for each of my brothers and me.

However, she also belonged to the neighborhood network of older women whose private passion was catching me and/or my brothers in some type of mischievous behavior. Everybody in our neighborhood knew each other's most intimate activities. The worst of it was that what they did not know for sure, I think they made up. You have to remember, there was only one station on the television and most people in my neighborhood were lucky to even have a television, so entertainment was in great demand.

Also a member in that infamous ring was Miss Dot Tawes, who lived on the opposite side of our house. Mom would send us to Miss Dot's house to get fresh eggs and rainwater from her indoor cistern. Dad said that rainwater made the best coffee.

It was as if neighbors like Miss Addie and Miss Dot were positioned intricately throughout the neighborhood to maximize visibility of our activities. It was Miss Dot who was at her post when my brother and I set the backyard field on fire. But, that is another story.

From her rocking chair on the front porch Miss Addie could see everything that took place across the street or in our front yard. On this one sunny summer afternoon I was returning from a trip to Archie Tyler's store across the street. I failed to pay proper attention to traffic and ran out in front of a vehicle traveling down Richardson Avenue.

Now, bear in mind that to get to Archie Tyler's store I had to cross Richardson Avenue, travel across a major railroad track and then make my way across Maryland Avenue. So, it was a trip that included my need to maneuver across the two major highways in and out of Crisfield and the very busy railroad tracks that led to the seafood plants along the water. So, I think running out in front of a car was minimal compared to what dangers potentially lurked along my path.

But, Miss Addie saw the whole thing. The screeching brakes of the car brought my mother rushing to our front porch like she had been shot out of cannon. The minute my mother reached the porch she had no time to assess what had happened before Miss Addie began yelling, "I saw it all.

He nearly got killed. I would beat him. Beat him because he almost got killed."

Of course Mom was faced with having Miss Addie's judgment call made clearly for all to hear. So, in order to keep face with the community and show that she worried about me, she did just what Miss Addie suggested. She beat me like a dirty rug. By the time she got done with me I had wished several times I had been struck by the car. Oh well, I guess that it does take a village to raise a child.

Filthy, nasty and mean

As Dad and my uncle hoisted the monstrosity up through the back screen door and onto the porch Mom's eyes were aglow. She could have been no happier and proud if she were being named Miss Crustacean.

What brought this joy to my mother? It was a second-hand wringer-type washer and it spelled the end of washing clothes in a galvanized wash tub and wringing them out by hand; household chores that were just one step up from hauling clothes down to the creek and scrubbing them on a washboard.

The washer had a great big white cylinder belly with what looked like two rolling pins slowly turning above. The idea was to take the clothes out of the big tub and one by one run them through the two spinning tubes which resulted in having the excess water squeezed out so the clothes could then be hung on the clothes line.

It was still an arduous task and Mom found that draining the water from the tub and filling it up again took so much time that she would often wash several loads of clothes in the same water. By the time she had finished washing our clothes the laundry water was so gray and thick with dirt you could shovel it out with a spade.

When I recall growing up in the 60s, I think about how Mom and Dad had it compared to today's household standards. The washing of clothes is but one example. We had no indoor bathroom or hot water plumbing, so you can imagine raising three heathen young'uns could be a massive chore of its own.

Dirt was to us what white is to snow. There were few times after 7 a.m. that you would not find us looking like we had been in a turd fight. There were but a few words that were used on a routine basis to describe the Windsor young'uns – "filthy", "nasty" and "mean."

I can't recall how many times a week we were given full-fledged baths. However, I do recall that in the winter Mom would bathe us one at a time in the kitchen where the most heat could be found in any one room. Often she would light the kitchen cook stove and drop the oven door to make sure it stayed warm enough.

One by one, we would be hoisted up on a kitchen chair and scrubbed from head to toe. Mom would comb our head with a lice comb and it felt like she was scraping out a half-inch of scalp. She must have done a pretty good job because I cannot recall any of us ever getting head lice.

As one young'un was being disinfected, the other two would be sitting in chairs waiting their turn. The bath water was heated on the stove and dumped in a wash basin, so it would get cold if we were not sitting there ready to take our turn. Of course it was the job of the two sitting on deck to try and make the one getting washed laugh or fidget around. This would make Mom mad and result in her thrashing us with whatever was in her hand at the time. The usual implement was a wet wash cloth. There was nothing more painful than a wet wash rag being slapped against wet, bare skin, especially when Mom was no more than a few inches away.

Summer was a little easier because we would get washed in a big gray galvanized tub that sat on the back porch, or sometimes in the back yard. Mom would have to heat the bath water on the stove and tote it out to the tub, so you can imagine it was one tub full of water per three young'uns.

This had to have been somewhat of a source of entertainment for folks in the neighborhood, including family members who dropped by and had to walk right past one or two of us sitting naked in the wash tub. As I tried feverishly to cover all of my 2,000 body parts there was little you could do but wave as they passed by.

Of course I was usually the last to get a bath and by the time my two brothers had got out of the tub the water was so thick and dark it was like I was sitting in a bucket of tar. There was enough sand on the bottom of the tub to backfill a construction site. I am not sure how my head got washed because I would just as soon have shoved my head into an outhouse hole as dunk it in that bath water after my two brothers were finished.

Looking back I have little doubt that Mom and Dad had a lot more to deal with when it came to routine household chores.

Fighting over the 'Wish Book'

There is something about Christmas that creates an automatic sense of nostalgia. I think for me it's the toys in the department stores and the advertisements on television. I guess I come from the "Wish Book" generation. It was the arrival of the Sears & Roebuck "Wish Book" catalogue that confirmed to me and my brothers that Christmas was really on its way.

The book became the most prized possession in the Windsor household. My older brother, Tommy, and I would actually fight over the use of it. You would have thought that we felt destined to receive every item in the book's toy section. That catalogue had an extreme impact on my life growing up in Crisfield. It is amazing, but I can actually recall several of the covers for the annual Wish Book.

It used to be mailed to our household, I guess until Sears & Roebuck realized how much mailing that catalogue to households cost. By then I am sure Sears moguls realized every kid in America would crawl on hands and knees through a bed of glass to make sure the book was at their house by Christmas.

I think back on the toys that were listed in the Wish Book and realize how by today's standards they would equate to a woodstove in the opinions of our modern day youth. But, those toys still make me smile, because they seemed so magical on the pages of the Wish Book. I can still remember how determined I was to get the "Rock'em Sock'em Robots" as my Christmas present. These two square-jawed boxers seemed so exciting to me. I would see the television commercial where these two kids are aggressively pumping the manual thumb controls on these red and blue robots and all of a sudden the winner is determined as the red robot's head pops up off his shoulder. Had to have it!

As kids we were allowed to look through the Wish Book and pick three toys that we really hoped to get, and out of those Mom and Dad would convince "Santa" to get us one of them. Of course I could always count on my traditional under the tree toys as well – a "Slinky," "Etch a Sketch" and "Cootie Bugs." I still cannot understand why anyone would celebrate head lice with a take-a-part toy.

Furthermore, I cannot believe how gullible and bored we young people must have been that we would become desirous of an oversized spring. I know that Slinky looked neat on television, but that was because the kids playing with that must have lived in a fire tower with stairs. The Slinky would move end over end down those stairs. If you did not have a set of stairs in your house like the Governor Ross Mansion you were in for a big disappointment. You can only move Slinky so long from hand to hand before it becomes more like work than play.

I eventually got my "Rock'em Sock'em Robots." Man, was I ecstatic! I think I got the robots the same year my brother Tommy got a chemistry set and a rock collection kit. I guess it would not have taken Dr. Phil long to figure out which one of us was destined for academic and career success.

I bet there are actually some people my age who still have their childhood toys. Somewhere somebody about 50 years old still possesses a 1960s circa "GI Joe" or a full set of the original "Hot Wheels" track and cars.

Well, unfortunately, by the time summer had arrived, there was only one robot which still had its head. I can remember playing with it and you would know when the blue robot won because the metal rod, void of a head, would pop up. My cootie bugs had only about two or three legs each and Slinky had been stretched to the point it was now a straight piece of metal.

Oh well, I always knew the Sears & Roebuck "Wish Book" would be coming next fall!

'Miss Sally' was too invasive

I think I was six years old before I realized I was not the only person in the world named "Tony." I know I wasn't aware of it in 1962 when I was completely awe struck as I was watching "Romper Room" on television and "Miss Sally" said she could see me as she gazed through her "Magic Mirror." I remember it like it was yesterday.

She was gazing through her "Magic Mirror" and chanting, "Romper stomper, bomper boo, tell me, tell me, tell me do. Magic Mirror tell me today did all my friends have fun at play? I see Donny, and Leslie and Peter and Tony." That is when I dropped my sandwich and ran through the house like Grant through Richmond. I would probably not have been quite so shocked, but at the time I was sitting on the couch eating a peanut butter and jelly sandwich in my underwear. I suppose I should have been more prepared because every morning at the end of the show she would look through the "Magic Mirror" and then name off the first name of at least 20 kids that she could see. I should have been concerned that she might one day see me and therefore I should be sitting in front of the television in a little more than my underwear.

It's amazing how much of an imagination you can have when you have not yet been polluted by the cynicism of society. I mean this woman was looking through a mirror that had no glass in it. She just held and empty frame in front of her face and chanted and there was no doubt in my mind, or the minds of anybody else watching the show that she could see us. It was like Captain Kangaroo. He carried

165

on conversations with Mr. Moose and Mr. Bunny and I thought they were real animals. The youthful mind is awesome. However, as a child I progressed and began to separate fantasy from reality. For instance, it was a fantasy that I would continue to sit around on the sofa watching television and eating peanut butter and jelly sandwiches in my underwear. There was going to be more expected of me as I added the years to my age.

I was fortunate. As a child my father woke each morning before the sun came up and chopped and stacked firewood, fed and milked the cows, hand-shucked horse corn for feed and gathered eggs; all this prior to the school day.

Since we did not live on a farm when I was growing up, the expectations my father had for me were somewhat limited and fundamental. The most basic expectation was "go to school" and "do the best you can do." I think I pretty much accomplish those goals throughout the first six or seven years of my school career. I think outside of a few collisions over attitude, a smart mouth and fighting with my brothers, Dad and I kept an even pace with limited tension.

However, it was in those high school days that I began to learn a new and exciting lesson about reality; that lesson being "dad don't play." I had come to recognize that most all my physical confrontations with Dad were relegated to the home front and not school.

I guess I carried a false sense of security, believing that Dad was less aggressive when it came to my behavior in school. This was definitely a fantasy; however, that was something I was destined to learn the hard way. Actually most lessons I learned as a child came the hard way. I was a scholar and Dean's List recipient at the "School of Hard Knocks."

But, you would think having experienced Dad's wrath at home, I would be cautious about doing things at school that would in any way risk firing up his very sensitive temper. Nope. I for some reason had a death wish. As a teenager I became the teacher's worst nightmare and the vice-principal's constant companion.

I found more interest in being "Class Clown" and less in striving to be a class success. As much fun as this daily stage act in the classroom was, I often found less than popular reviews when I arrived home to find that a teacher had issued complaint to my father. This is when I would more than a few times, perform my second stage show which was as lead dancer in Dad's well-choreographed "belt ballet."

Oh well, there is much to be said about improvisation.

Graduate of 'School of Hard Knocks'

I took the proverbial walk down memory lane over this past weekend. I found myself in my hometown of Crisfield on Saturday and after driving down by Brick Hill, near the American Legion, I drove to my old elementary school. Though the property is now less sand, dirt and grass and more concrete and blacktop, the building and grounds remain pretty much the way they were in the 1960s.

I attended Crisfield Elementary # 1 from 1963 until 1968. After that the city made its first move to integration, well behind the national trend, and I attended 7th grade at Woodson Junior High School, which had previously served as the lone school for the community's black students.

There is something pristine about my memories of Crisfield Elementary # 1. Whenever I think about those days my memories are reminiscent of innocence; though I am sure I was far from innocent of the traditional childhood buffoonery that comes with being a young boy with little in the way of entertainment at his disposal.

On Saturday the playground in the front and rear of the school seemed so much smaller as I walked over that same ground which at one time housed a major part of my young world. This was where my social life existed. It was the place I came each day to see more than just the one friend I had back at home.

But, as I purposely stood in the same spots as I did as an elementary student, I wondered how much more successful I would have been if I had taken it all so much more seriously. As I grow older and experience much more of life, I regret that I did not commit myself more totally to school. I mean, I graduated from high school and today I am even going to college. However, by the time I decided to give college a shot, I was old enough to die. I find myself hearing Dad's all familiar verbal drill ringing in my head some days. It would always come right after I got my report card. For me this was a dismal time around my house.

My older brother Tommy would come home with a report card that was so good that when he brought it into the room it shimmered and I heard a choir sing. Dad would take the report card from my brother, fully aware that he was about to witness true genius documented. After he gave Tommy the customary, "Good job, bunk," he would turn to me. The look he would give me as he waited for me to hand him my report card was much like the look of school custodian who was about to take on the job of cleaning up a clogged toilet.

I was always reluctant to give him my report card. I would consider losing it on the way home from school, or maybe telling him that I had been attacked on the way home and my report card stolen. But, I knew all of these would only delay the pending misery.

So, I would throw a big smile on my face and hand Dad the report card. I think there were actually times when Dad would hope that he would look at the report card and find that I had finally "buckled down" and made the grade. NOT.

He would look at the report card and say almost the same thing he had said when he got the last report card, "Son, it would be different if I thought this was as good as you could do. But, you are an A or B student." Then he would throw in that line that really stung, "You are actually smarter than your brother, Tommy." Who was he kidding? Albert Einstein could have taken classes under my brother, Tommy. I knew my brother Tommy and I was no Tommy Windsor. I was certainly smart enough to realize that.

I certainly was not smart enough to take advantage of the learning opportunities of school. My presence in the classroom was much like a running generator motor during a power outage; it has to be there, but nobody wants to hear it. When I wasn't acting like a drunken ape, I was asleep. You always hear about teachers waking sleeping students with a tap on the shoulder or on his or her desk. In my case, I would not be surprised to find that some of my teachers found a way to secretly drug me and induce an hour long coma. I would fall asleep in class and when I would wake up the classroom would be empty. That would not have been so concerning to me, except it was during a fire drill. I guess I was not always the most popular person in school. I remember my 10th grade typing teacher wrote in my yearbook that I was the Most Likely to wind up in a rehab.

But, as my Uncle Stanford once said, "There are those of us who graduate from high school and others of us who graduate from the 'school of hard knocks.' I am a certified, honors student graduate of the School of Hard Knocks. There is no greater or more ruthless teacher, than life itself.

Those of us who choose to treat the gift of school and education as nothing more than a social gathering and a captive audience for our buffoonish side shows, will one day "pay the piper." I have so many times wished that I had actually listened and participated in the classroom experience. I have no doubt life would have been much easier and though I am happy with the several jobs I hold, things could have run much smoother. Now, in hindsight, I think Dad was right. I probably was an A or B student; I just lacked the most important source of knowledge – common sense.

My life at the Haunted Manor

Boooooo! Did I scare you?

Sorry, it seems to run in my family. I sometimes think I grew up in a house of horrors. My parents are wonderful people and have always been great parents. They raised five successful children. But, at one time, there was a dark side to my parents. You see, they seemed to thrive on scaring the beejeebers out of their children. My father was the ringleader. He had a knack for hiding behind a piece of furniture and jumping out at you with a banshee scream as you walked by.

I think he must have been a contortionist, because he had the ability to hide behind any sized piece of furniture. I think I remember him hiding behind a broom one time. It got so that I was scared to walk through the house. I never knew when he would lunge out. It was like living in the *House on Haunted Hill.*

Even today, I am half-scared to open the basement door, or a kitchen cabinet, for fear that my father is waiting on the other side. My father's high pitched, shrill scream was also a favorite during a scary movie. It would always come at the precise moment that the movie was breaking for commercial. When the screen went black, just a split second before the commercial started, my father would let out that horrible, freakish scream.

But it was not just my father that had an appetite for sadistic torment. My mother was no slouch yourself. Where my father used no props, simply utilizing his superb sense of timing and a set of great circumstances, my mother combined a likewise, grand sense of timing accompanied by special effects. Many was the night that I would walk past the screened back door, or look out of a dark living room window and find my mother's contorted face, pressed against the screen or glass; her head covered with a pair of nylon stockings.

The nylon stocking gag was an inexpensive way to create horror, and gave old pantyhose an alternative use after they had runs and were otherwise ready for the trash. However, on special occasions, my mother would pull out all stops and bring to life the "Freddy Krueger" of my young life – "Booger Jacob."

My brothers and I have the utmost respect for Booger Jacob because we never knew when he would appear. For Booger Jacob's visit, my mother had to enlist the help of my grandmother. My grandmother would wait until my brothers and I were playing in the living room floor and totally unaware of our surroundings. "Hush, hush," she would say in a low, almost eerie tone. "Do you hear that noise?"

Our eyes would immediately become as big around as a pair of television satellite dishes. We would then scamper onto the arms of my grandmother's chair, almost climbing on top of her. Then it would happen. From an old closet under the stairway, my mother would seemingly float out, covered from head to toe in a white sheet with a grotesque green mask over her face. She would linger there for a few seconds and then go back into the closet, leaving my brother and me gasping for breath.

Today my parents find it hard to believe that they once did these kinds of things. I am keenly aware that they would never do this to their grandchildren. Oh well, I guess we were just lucky.

More than a man with a belt

We celebrated my father's birthday this past weekend. The majority of his five children were present and we joined our parents for a cookout. For some reason I cannot remember anyone's birthday including my own. My younger brother makes it a point to call me on several occasions to remind me when my parents' birthdays are coming.

This past Saturday was my father's actual birthday. Because of my lapse in memory, rather than invite my father out to dinner on his birthday, I instead invited him to bring his pickup truck to my house and help me haul trash to the dump. I felt really bad because of all the things my father has done for me over the years you would think I could at least remember his birthday.

I tried to remember all of the headaches that I caused my father as I was growing up. There were so many things to remember that it caused me to have a headache, so I stopped thinking about it. I was by no means the most cooperative child to deal with.

Of course my father prided himself on having learned the art of discipline from the "old school." If you combine old-fashioned philosophy with his years in the military, serving as a sergeant in the Army in Korea, and his career as a police officer, you have the makings of "Hitler with a belt." That was the way I saw my father as I was growing up. I recognize that this was not a true perception of this man I called Dad. He was strict because he loved us and did not want to see us as the victims of a cruel world; yeah, this and we also got on his nerves.

It amazes me how off often my brothers and I could get on my father's nerves. You would think we would recognize the key moments when it was not wise to make a racket in the house. This was usually just once a day, every day, all day long.

But, most important, never make noise while Dad is watching the news. You would only hear him utter the word "hush" no more than twice and then when you least expected it - expect it. I think Dad has a place in history books as being the quickest and most precise when it came wielding a 32-inch, black, leather belt. As I said in the past my father did not abuse us. We always got what we deserved; unfortunately, we deserved it so often it seemed like abuse.

I had the ignorant approach to things that led me to push my father. Even if he were in a good mood, I would push him into a bad one. Like the time I had my ear pierced and tried to hide it from my very conservative father. I had let my hair get long and was able to cover the earring.

Unfortunately, one day I decided to lie down and take a nap before dinner. When I came to the dinner table I was unaware that my hair had gotten disheveled and my earring was showing. Looking out of the corner of his eye my father abruptly asked, "What's that in your ear?" I immediately responded, "It's an earring." Suddenly I had a sense of defiance; a sense of pride. I was going to stand by my principals and not surrender to the fear my father's wrath.

My sudden burst of defiance lasted less than a minute. It quickly faded as my father got up from the kitchen table and retrieved a pair of pliers from a nearby cabinet. I quickly fumbled to take the earring out of my ear as I saw Dad, pliers in hand, making his way toward my head. I had no doubt that Dad was prepared to yank the earring out of my ear, possibly starting from the other side of my head.

However, in all fairness, along with the discipline, my father also made sure our family always had food on the table, clothes on our backs and a name we could be proud of. On the occasion of my father's birthday I take this opportunity to answer some of his more frequently asked questions.

"Yes, I thought you were heating all outdoors." Yes, I thought you were "made of money." And yes, "if my friends jumped off a bridge, so would I."

A case for year-round school

I can sense summertime coming. The warm air and sunny skies bring back memories of growing up in the marshlands of the Eastern Shore. As summer approached it was hard to concentrate because we knew school would be out for three months. It seems to me that kids today get out of school more often than we did. Maybe that is just a perception.

One thing is for sure, it was no easy task to expect school to close because of inclement weather. I can remember a time before my hometown had a municipal waste water line out to our area of town. The tide would come up so high that water would come into the kitchen. I can remember seeing water rats and black snakes swimming up to the porch. It was like a ghetto Noah's Ark.

But, no matter how high the water got, we still had school. I guess they figured if the kids from Smith Island could catch the boat over to Crisfield every morning, it should be no problem for us. Even in the winter, it could snow so high we couldn't see the top of the city water tank; still we had to make school somehow.

Summer was the only reprieve from school we had. It would not have done any good to call in a bomb threat. I remember when Stevie A. dropped a stink bomb in the heater system. Smoke poured out of every heater duct in the building. Classrooms were gassed with the aroma of what smelled like putrid animal flesh. Gagging students were met by custodians who simply opened the sliding classroom windows and turned on stand up fans while teachers herded the students back to class like victims of the Los Angeles riots. Class resumed.

This was the same when Johnny A. urinated on that same heater system. It was wintertime and every heater was blazing and blowing. It wasn't long before the entire school smelled like Big Foot's underarms. Still classes went on.

I guess our school staff knew they were dealing with a horde of hairless apes when it came to the bunch of rope swingers that attended school in Crisfield. There was no sense in shutting school down when you could at least keep them off the streets for a few hours. I mean these were the same bunch of hell raisers who shoved "Skagg," the town drunk in to a clothes dryer at the Main Street Laundromat and turned it on. When police chief Carmine pulled him out of the dryer, he said it was the first time he ever saw Skagg walk straight.

I guess I shouldn't paint all my childhood companions with such a broad brush of negativity. After all, it was me and Dennis Morgan who played Steppenwolf's "Pusher Man" from the steeple audio system at the Marion Baptist Church. Hidden behind bushes in the field where we had fled, we saw people running out of their houses like roaches under a kitchen light, trying to get to the church to silence the grinding guitars and less than endearing lyrics. Now, that was youthful ignorance and disrespect if I ever heard of it.

Man, if my young'un did something like that I would whoop him till child services came. Hmmm, as a matter of fact, that is exactly what dad did. Except child services never came. The only thing that kept the rest of the town from taking turns putting knots on my head was that dad didn't need any help.

Now that I think about it, I guess it is no wonder our community leaders were trying to keep us in school.

I could sense it was Christmas

As a young boy coming down the stairs the day after Thanksgiving, I would know right away it must be close to the "Christmas season." My father had gotten up and placed his country music Christmas albums on the stereo and they were filling the living room with holiday sounds.

For those younger folk who don't know what an album is, it is a black round disc which is about 10 times the size of a CD. My father's record player could stack several of these discs and then drop them one after the other. The needle would robotically drop to the first band on the album and play all selections before automatically starting the process again. I know that compared to today's technology that is a bit cumbersome, but you have to admit the whole process was quite impressive.

However, Dad had a state-of-the-art stereo, which actually meant he had a huge, walnut finished console that stretched across the room like a chest of drawers. The cabinet was about six-feet long, but the area that actually did all the work was probably less than half of that. Nonetheless, the country holiday music was something that signaled Christmas was really on its way. There were two other such signals that I would be waiting for and then I could be sure Christmas and Santa were within patience range.

One signal came while watching "Rudolph the Red-Nosed Reindeer," on television. When the program broke for a commercial, an animated Santa Claus was shown racing down the snowy mountainside riding a Norelco electric razor.

My childhood home was not decorated with store bought Christmas products like small artificial trees or Santa Claus knick-knacks, unless they had been passed down through at least two generations of family. But, the Christmas spirit could be developed through some homemade decorations, like the Christmas cards Mom taped up around the doors in the living room. At the time we must have gotten several hundred Christmas cards because the cards would be draped around doors and windows like garland.

The colorful holiday cards matched perfectly the comic books and newspapers Dad had wedged into the front door to keep out the draft. All of this was given a backdrop of windows with thick plastic stapled over them to protect our house from the winds of winter. Our living room looked like a flea market. Then there would be the plastic candelabras that had six lights. Traditionally, the lights were orange, but when they burned out Mom put any color light she had. We had candelabras with red, blue, green and yellow lights.

For some reason my father had a tradition that dictated that we could not put a Christmas tree up until Christmas Eve. Dad would always go out and cut the tree out of the woods himself. He would drag it home the afternoon of Christmas Eve and lean it up against the back of the house.

It was always a cedar tree. I have never understood why a cedar of all trees. It is the most ill shaped tree in the forest. It never resembled a tree in shape, just a mass of cedar needles. Those needles would fall off the tree and we would still be picking cedar needles out of our feet in July.

I guess my childhood home did not rate a spot in Better Homes & Gardens, but one thing is sure, it embodied the spirit of Christmas and the joy of family. I wish I would have appreciated that a little more at the time.

Never too hot to go outside

I hear a lot about "Global Warming" in the news. I cannot comment on the phenomena, whether it is real or myth; I simply do not have the expertise on the subject. But, I will say that as hot as it gets each year, I would have to stop short of saying that it is any warmer now than it was when I was growing up.

I can't recall the exact temperatures because memory does not allow an actual physical connection to the past. However, that does not stop me from knowing that summer in Crisfield as a young boy produced many days that I know were hotter than my grandmother's woodstove. I need only cast my mind back to those days and nights when I can remember sweating like an oil company CEO at a Senate hearing.

My mother and grandmother would sit on the front porch and hold prayer vigils asking Jesus for a breeze; all the while waving Bradshaw & Sons Funeral Home paper fans on a stick in front of their faces to try and stay cool.

I can remember Mom could have used an ice scraper to rake the dirt beads off the back of my neck. I guess as kids we never really considered that it would ever be too hot to play outside. I never heard anything about dehydration or exhaustion.

We never had to run around with plastic water bottles. Every house had an outside spigot and a hose. There was always the constant threat of "hoof and mouth disease" being levied at us from parents and teachers when we drank after one another at the school water fountain. That must not have been too frightening to any of us because we would wrap our lips around the end of a garden hose or the mouth of the metal spigot like we were being fitted for dentures.

No, drinking after one another was never done in a cautious way. I can remember sitting in the side yard with my best friend Carey. We must have been about four years old. He had a Tootsie Roll and ate it before I could complain about his unwillingness to share. I guess I got to his conscience, because after chewing the Tootsie Roll into an unrecognizable mash of chocolate, he spit it into my eagerly awaiting mouth. It was actually much easier to eat the second time around. It was only later that we learned to consider that type of activity "gross."

We also had no air conditioning at school or home; however, we knew nothing of the comfort of air conditioning so I suppose we had no idea what we were missing. The only thing we could do was sweat, and sweat we did. By the end of a day outside playing with my friends I must have gone through more water than Noah.

After sweating and rolling around on the ground in the dirt and grass, when I came in the house I must have looked like a walking village hut. I would get a bath and then go to bed and sweat some more. It seemed that whatever breeze may happen to be blowing it was always blowing on the opposite side of the house.

This is when Dad would put on his mechanical engineering hat and begin to put into place his theory of wind control. He would take the huge window fan that we were given by my Uncle Oscar and Aunt Evelyn, and put it in my bedroom window backwards, so the fan would be blowing outside, instead of into the bedroom.

He would then run downstairs and at the base of our stairwell, open the doorway which led into the living room.

Then he would open the front and back doors. Afterwards he would come back to our bedroom. We would be mesmerized as he related to us the "scientific process" which would cause the fan in my window to create a sucking air. This would pull the air from downstairs up through the rest of the house and into our bedroom as it was pushed outside by the fan.

By the time he was done explaining the mass engineering phenomena he had put in place, we were asleep, and so it really didn't matter anyway. He would then retire to his bedroom and climb in bed with a box fan blowing air on him and Mom. Of course in this case, the fan was actually blowing in the right direction. Oh well, I could always count on Dad to make sure he did everything possible to prepare for this hard, often cruel world. So, in preparing us for life without air conditioning, perhaps Dad actually knew in our lifetime we would be faced with "global warming." Hmmmm. That is an interesting concept.

My dad when he got back from serving in Korea.
We believed those eyes had special powers.

He always found the truth

It was as if he was peering into my very soul. His eyes piercing mine like beams from an x-ray machine. Beads of sweat began forming at the base of my scalp and I was unsteady on my feet. It would have been totally traumatic, except while doing it he was standing in the living room in his boxer shorts.

It was Dad's fool proof way to tell if his young'uns were telling the truth. "Let me look in your eyes," he would say. Then he would stare intently into my pupils and even if I was totally innocent and telling the truth, I would get so nervous that I would look as guilty as a donut thief with a powder mustache.

Actually Dad's process seemed quite accurate. It was either that it was accurate or I was always lying. I did not realize it at the time, but whenever Dad did his "looking in the eyes" thing, it meant he was not actually going to take any physical action. It was just his way to make us be convinced that he could dig the truth out of our very skull.

You see, with Dad there was very little warning, if any at all. As I have said countless times before, while Dad was serving in Korea, he must have also trained as a Ninja warrior. He could take his belt off, whoop us and have his belt back on and buckled before we had a chance to cry.

But, with Dad there was always a sense of mystique. It was not necessarily that he had to convince us that he knew our every move, because he did. He must have had a network of people assigned to telling him when his young'uns were acting like heathens. The dinner table was more like a Catholic confessional. He would look down at his plate and slowly and methodically begin to share all that he knew of our actions for the day or past week.

It was not long before I would try to cut him off by making sure I was able to confess my transgressions before he got to my list of meanness. I think as a young boy I was convinced that Dad knew as much about what I was doing when no one was around as Jesus.

But, it was not always the bad things that Dad took the time to know about. I recall in the second grade I had forgotten to tell my parents that there was an Antrim Bureau assembly at school and it cost 25 cents to go. I got to school and as Miss McCready collected everybody's quarter I sat sad and so upset that I did not remind my Mom and Dad about that show. Now, I would be sitting in the classroom by myself, with my head on my desk while everybody else enjoyed seeing a man showing and talking about snakes of the eastern United States.

I was feeling so down and then Miss McCready came to my desk and said, "Oh, Tony, your Dad stopped by school and brought your assembly money." I could not have been happier if she had announced that I was going to a shopping spree at the toy store in the upstairs of Kaufman's Furniture. But, that was my Dad; he knew everything about his young'uns.

Dead insects became artwork

It was stunning and added such class to my childhood home. Hanging in the living room, in a corner that during the winter was reserved for our annual cedar Christmas tree, was our fly strip. This household item looked like a slick, dangling, twisted piece of yellow duct tape. The thing that made it even more adorable was the many flies, mosquitoes and occasional moth that were stuck to it like mini wall ornaments.

I cannot fathom that we actually counted on the fly strip as a means of insect control. It was ugly. Not only was it ugly, but it was also disgusting. The insects that were stuck to the glue of this strip were still alive, struggling to get free.

I recall that a gas station near my home starting making fly strips available in a more decorative packaging. Instead of the traditional twisted, yellowing tape that just hung there, these strips were enclosed in a box that revealed the strip through several golden windows.

Yes, Dad came home proudly carrying these new fly strips. These were so bright and colorful that we actually hung them over our kitchen table. How appetizing. These long, narrow boxes hung like Japanese box lights. The only difference between these and an oriental hanging lamp were the countless bugs that adhered to the strips, most stuck on their backs allowing their many legs to kick about. The bugs were totally exposed through the several window frames that did little to conceal the paraffin-looking strips and their helpless victims.

How could anyone ever consider that a fly strip, regardless of its packaging, would be a household decoration? I don't know, but I really think my mother and father thought these should hang right up there with pictures of me and my brothers. As a matter of fact, the fly strips were far more accessible to the eye than our Olan Mills portraits.

But, when I think back on it, I guess flies, moths, mosquitoes and the like were an intricate part of the household decorum. Very few times can I recall that there were any less than five to ten dead moths and flies curled up on the bottom of the plastic lamp shades that attached to the bulbs in our ceiling lights. The light bulb allowed a very graphic silhouette of the grave yard of bugs that lay on the bottom of the shades.

Once the dead bug carcasses reached a depth making it worth the effort to use a kitchen chair to retrieve the plastic lamp shade, Mom would bring it down, dump out the dead bugs and wash the lamp shade. It would then be placed back serving more as a coffin than a lamp shade.

There were also the many mosquitoes that fluttered about in the living room while we tried to watch television. These varmints would pitch on us one by one. They were barely visible to the naked eye. That is until they had sucked several pints of blood from each one of us. Then they could be seen beating up against the living room wall, huge blood-filled bellies that kept them from rising much more than a few feet off the floor.

Someone would always end up striking one or more of the mosquitoes, causing the blood to shoot from their bellies and create bloody artwork spattered across the living room walls. Cleaning up this mess ranked right up there with emptying the bug laden lamp shades in terms of Mom's appreciation for this type of housework.

Thankfully we now have more civilized forms of insect control in our homes today, like the bug zapper that electrocutes the unsuspecting creatures. But, believe it or not, I have actually seen fly strips hanging from a ceiling or two in recent years. I suppose it must be the antique appeal.

Why I am afraid of flying

I was born with a fear of flying. I have no idea how this fear originated, but for some reason I just always correlated flying with something horrific.

I recall a number of years ago while working as the Editor of a local newspaper, Sgt. Gary Flood of the Seaford Police Department, made me aware of a really nice human interest story. He explained to me that a little five-year-old girl had become infatuated with a member of the parachute group who had taken part in the recent police department's "Night Out Against Crime." The little girl, Trina Moore, spent the evening following this parachutist around, "helping" him load his chute and watching as he floated to the ground during his parachute jump.

The Seaford Police Department and representatives of the Laurel Airport decided to take this little girl's excitement to another level and invited her to accompany her favorite parachutist while he made one of his jumps. Sgt. Flood invited me to come to the airport and cover this event for the newspaper. It was a great idea, so I agreed. I recall pulling up in the airport parking lot as several police officers, including Flood, waited with Trina and her parents, Floyd and Bonnie Moore for the plane to be ready for flight.

I performed the traditional reporter duties, including interviewing Trina and her parents to document the excitement this little girl was experiencing. I thanked Sgt. Flood for inviting the paper to the event and told him as soon as the plane landed I would again interview Trina and get her reaction to being up in the airplane. Realizing that I was not intending to make the flight myself, Sgt. Flood immediately used my dedication to good reporting as a tool to pry me into the airplane. "The real story is going to be that little girl's face when she is up inside that plane," he said. I bit on Sgt. Flood's line like a bulldog on a three-pound steak. That was my first mistake.

Before I knew it I was fitted with a parachute and shoved into the airplane like a bag of mail. The passenger seat had been removed and it was decided that this would be the ideal location for me and my picture-taking duties. The space I was allocated was minimal and with the huge parachute on my back I was wedged into my spot like a 20-pound turkey stuffed in a 10-pound bag.

The plane engine started and we began coasting down the runway. If I had wanted to make a last second jump from the plane it would have taken six men and a Hurst Tool to pry me out of my makeshift seat. As the plane left the ground I knew it was too late; I was now face to face with my greatest fear.

Shortly into flight I finally resigned myself to making the best of my predicament. Just as I started feeling somewhat normal, the pilot looked at me and said, "Let's have some fun. This little girl is going to love this," he said. All of a sudden, the pilot took the plane straight up and shoved the throttle. The plane was immediately transformed into a rocket. We were traveling so fast that I felt the flesh on my face flatten to my skull and I think my forehead was pushed to somewhere around the back of my neck.

Unfortunately, instead of becoming excited, Trina began to scream as the plane shot upwards. The pilot, realizing he had to calm the little girl, suddenly directed the plane toward the ground and shoved the throttle and we were plummeting toward the ground so fast that I saw Jesus. It was horrific!

I began to feel sick. I became so ill that I broke out into a sweat and thought I would explode at any minute. Suddenly, someone shouted that the door was open and it was as if the entire side of the airplane disappeared. I was immediately staring at wide open spaces and the ground 10,000 feet below.

Five parachutists stepped out onto the wing of the plane and within seconds had disappeared into mid air. I tried to take pictures, but I was so nauseaus that it was all I could do to hold my camera. I was so sick that for a brief time I considered leaping out of the open airplane door.

Finally, the pilot started navigating the plane toward earth. When we touched ground the doors of the plane opened and everyone jumped out, leaving me still jammed inside. I was so sick I could barely move. I shifted my weight around until me and the parachute rolled out of the door and onto the ground below.

I lay on the ground in a heap like a bag of roadside trash. I crawled on hand and knees to a nearby tree stump and Floyd Moore helped me get out of my parachute. The sweat literally poured off of me and my face was as white as rice. I was helped to my car by Floyd, who followed closely behind me as I drove toward home.

I recall that I crawled into the house and passed out in the living room floor. I was awaken a few hours later by my cat that was licking on my face. No doubt the cat thought she had stumbled onto 250 pounds of fresh kill. It was 10:30 p.m. before I actually began to feel anywhere near alive.

I have flown several times since my first flight out of Laurel Airport, all successfully and without a bad experience. However, my first flight experience will be something that I will never forget. I will also never forget Sgt. Gary Flood, the question is, can I ever forgive him? (Just kidding).

'Class Clown' is no classy title

I have a nephew who recently started school and it seems he has a propensity for trouble. He is a very intelligent, friendly child, but seems to possess a desire to fill the role of the Class Clown. Being described as the Class Clown seems harmless in and of itself; but trust me; I know what I am talking about when I say that this can be the single most destructive element of a child's education.

I do not speak as a child psychologist; I speak as a former, now retired, class clown. My classroom antics were so classic "clown," my mother should have named me "Bozo." I could have opened a Class Clown school. It was a tragic component of my academic career.

When my mother took me school shopping she should have been looking for big, floppy shoes, a polka dot jumpsuit and red hair. I am not sure my sister and brother in-law truly understand the commitment that goes into being the "Class Clown."

I am not talking about the children who go to school and get in trouble for fighting, backtalk, talking too much in class or not doing their school work. These are not the traditional "clowns."

The "Class Clown" is in a category of his or her own. The Class Clown stops at nothing to be center of attention and is on a mission to make other classmates laugh, or simply be amazed at what lengths they will go to be a buffoon.

The most concerning element of being a Class Clown comes from the almost innate desire to be the classroom entertainer, at the risk of facing the guaranteed wrath of your parents when the teacher has had enough of your classroom antics.

I knew without question that whenever the school called or wrote a note home about my cartoonish, Jerry Lewis-type charades, I could count on having in no way amused my father. When it came to my job as Class Clown, he had no sense of humor. Dad tired quickly of my classroom standup routine. It was so frustrating to my father that instead of going to school to get an education, his middle son treated the classroom like it was a stage at the LA Comedy Club. Yet, I would risk having my father beat me like a dusty rug, and continue my comedy tour.

The problem with being a Class Clown is that it is not as innocent a behavior as the title may infer. The Class Clowns are so determined to solicit a laugh from their audience that they not only endanger their chances of acquiring academic success, but can easily take the audience down with them.

I do not speak lightly when I use the word "determined." It seems that once seeing that you have the power to make a classmate laugh, it becomes addictive; you love the attention and, like a comedian, you start building on your routine to hopefully build on the classes reactions. For a short time, you are legendary in the classroom and your fellow classmates look to you to break up the oftentimes mundane, boring classroom environment.

But, trust me, the Class Clown, like most comedians and celebrities, has his or her run. Eventually your classmates will tire of your antics and even in some cases start to resent you as a distraction. They, unlike you, are deterred when facing unhappy parents because instead of concentrating on their school work, they paid unnecessary attention to the dunce stacking the classroom book supplies on top of the closet while the teacher is at the blackboard.

Hopefully my nephew learns quickly that the life of the Class Clown is not as exciting and rewarding as it now seems. Take it from someone who knows, all those times I made myself center of attention, everybody really was laughing at me, not with me.

My Aunt Lillian was a large woman, but sweet and gentle. Still, the snake would have been no match for her.

No big deal, it's just a snake

What could have been horrific enough to have caused my Aunt Lillian to race across the yard like an eight-point buck in bow season? Only a snake could incite this type of fear in my Aunt Lillian Tyler. I believe in her day, Aunt Lillian would have spit in Hitler's face and wrestled Satan. I can recall the story she told me as a young boy about the day she came upon the "Black Runner."

According to Aunt Lillian, she was working in the yard, oblivious to any other entity outside of the trees and birds. All of a sudden she came upon something that looked to be an old bicycle inner tube lying discarded in the yard. Closer inspection revealed a living, breathing, slithering snake. She claims the snake coiled up like a cobra and stood 6 feet tall.

Aunt Lillian immediately turned and ran like a dollar store stocking. As she headed across the yard, she momentarily looked back over her shoulder, only to be faced with what would now be her second biggest fear the snake was running behind her. My Aunt Lillian was a large woman, not fat, just large. She must have stood over 6-feet and weighed in at 230 pounds. But her large framed did not slow her down. She charged across the yard like Bigfoot in a forest fire.

According to Aunt Lillian, she reached the house, threw open the screened door and leaped inside. Standing inside, looking out the door, Aunt Lillian swore that the snake had jumped up and got his fangs stuck in the screened door and was hanging on to the door like a bulldog on a hambone.

My aunt was a good, Christian woman and I believe her story. But, if nothing else, it shows the degree that even the heartiest souls are scared of a snake. Growing up it was the snake stories that captivated everybody, young and old. No matter how much they feared even the thought of happening upon one of these reptiles, people still love to hear from those who did.

My father never feared snakes, having killed his share after they got into the hen house. However, my mother remains deathly afraid of the serpents. So, of course this provided my father with much recreational pleasure during the summer months. He would kill black snakes in the chicken house, or out in the backyard, and then bring the dead carcass into the house, hidden behind his back.

He would then find my mother innocently washing dishes or cooking dinner. Walking up to her he would nonchalantly mention that he found something lying around in the yard. He would then bring the limp, motionless snake out from behind his back and shake it in my mother's face.

She would, without hesitation, drop whatever she had in her hands, including my baby brother, and run screaming and wailing into the closest room with a door. No matter how many times my dad did this, it had the same reaction. It didn't matter that Dad always brought in a dead snake.

I mean, this snake could have been wearing an overcoat and sunglasses with a sign that read "This snake is dead. It is totally harmless." It was a snake and dead or alive, my mother has always been petrified of these serpents. Of course, my dad did little to relieve her fears. That would have damaged his ability to have fun.

This showed me two things. One, that the snake must be the most feared beast under 10 pounds and secondly, just how sadistic my family can be in the name of humor. Oh well, at least the chickens were being protected!

It is about the giver, not the gift

It lay on the counter top in Miss McCready's second grade classroom. It was rectangular, wrapped in paper covered with Santa Claus and his reindeer. It was my Christmas present. Each year in the first few levels of elementary school we would have a Christmas party. We would draw a name from a box and exchange gifts.

We waited with great anticipation as the days slowly passed to Christmas vacation. The last day was party day. It was like a warm up for the actual Christmas morning at home. Now, I am very quick to criticize some of today's young people for feeling so entitled and expecting lavish gifts throughout the year, especially at Christmas.

So, as I thought back on my own childhood, I certainly recognized that as much as I hate to admit it, I also felt somewhat entitled. However, this feeling of entitlement was offset greatly by the fact that my mother and father in no way found me to be entitled to anything except a bed, food and just enough clothes to keep me from going to school naked.

I thought about those school Christmas parties and suddenly realized that I had some issues that I wish I would have considered differently. For example, how about that Christmas present lying on the counter in Miss McCready's classroom that had my name on it. Today, I think about one of my classmate's parents going out to the store to buy an extra gift to give to some kid they didn't know from Adam's houseplant.

The fact is, growing up in the 1960s in Crisfield, Md., was not the hotbed of prosperity. Rich retirees were not coming to this crabbing village to while away their golden years in waterfront condos; there were farmers, waterman and small store owners by in large. So, in many cases, having one more gift to buy was a hardship.

But, being the traditional seven-year-old heathen rug rat, I became overwhelmed with what was inside that neatly wrapped Christmas gift and what benefit it would provide me. I pondered with great excitement what could be hidden inside that mysterious box. It was rectangular in shape, so it could be a myriad of possible things. Perhaps it was a board game? No, too small. Maybe it was a pair of pearl handled "Have Gun, Will Travel" revolvers? No, still too small.

As I pulled off the paper with the finesse of a wild bear in heat, I saw it. Oh, man, it was a crappy lifesavers book. It was 10 rolls of lifesavers stacked inside a box that opened like a book. I looked around and saw some girls playing with Barbie dolls and other guys racing Hot Wheels cars down the aisle beside my seat. Man, they were so lucky. I just stared at my book box with Santa Clause on the cover offering me a lifesaver. All these days of waiting and fantasizing over what gift I would get and I end up with a box of life savers. Woe is me.

This weekend I was in the checkout line of a local retail store. As I waited patiently in line, I spied something on the top shelf of a nearby end cap. It was a book of lifesavers. After all these years Santa Clause was still on the cover, offering anyone interested a lifesaver. I thought about how 46 years ago someone I did not know picked up a box of lifesavers just like this, included it in their store purchases, took it home and neatly wrapped it and wrote my name on it.

Perhaps it takes 46 years of being beat up by the real world and forced to realize that life is made up giving and receiving. This is not always just about giving and receiving the material things. It is about giving sincerely of your time and love to others and being willing to receive with gratitude, the offerings of thoughts and love from others.

I wish I could go back 46 years and re-open that small box of lifesavers and accept the true gift that was being given me – the gift of someone taking time for me. Now that I really think about it that was not such a crappy gift after all. Then again, no gift is.

My folks were good to their word

Growing up in Crisfield, Maryland in the 1960s, I seem to remember my mother or father having to tell me things over and over again. Why did they have to keep repeating the same instructions? Was it because they were particularly demanding, or was it perhaps because my head was as hard as an anvil? Let's see, what were some of those memorable remarks?

There is a vision of my mother standing at the kitchen mirror with a hairbrush in her hand. I can still see her drop the hairbrush to her side, bobby pins in her mouth, saying lovingly, "You're not going anywhere with me, looking like that!"

This of course meant that instead of actually washing up and brushing the stubble off my head, I had simply put on a different shirt and pants, not necessarily a clean shirt and pants, but different nonetheless. Sweat beads around my neck in a film of dirt mixed with sweat from head to toe made me look more like a modern art sculpture than a child.

Then there was winter. This was when my mother brought out her favorite words. She pulled them from the summer trunk, dusted them off and used them quite frequently during those cold winter days. "It's either in or out! If you come in that door and go out one more time I'm locking it and you will stay outside!" I guess at least once in my life I had to challenge my mother's warning and go outside that one last time. My mother, being a woman of her word, did just what she promised. The door locked and I went about my business. My father's black, nylon socks were my makeshift mittens and it took all of about two snowballs to leave them soaking wet.

So within, let's say, 55 seconds, my hands were frozen and I wanted in the house. I can only imagine the vision that appeared before my mother's eyes as I beat on the door, my face as red as Satan's drawers and hands feeling they were frostbitten. I don't know what hands feel like when there frostbitten but I'm sure it must be much like my hands felt at that time.

My mother was good to her word. In my mind there was no doubt that she was never going to open that door. With tears rolling down my face and frozen snot flying, I begged and pleaded, moaned and cried; to no avail. My mother was bound and determined that I would suffer her wrath for my role in breaking the sacred "winter door policy."

Looking back on my own job as a parent, I think I was not nearly as faithful to my words as my mother and father. I would threaten extreme punishments to my son, but usually, to avoid hearing the screams of dismay, I would back down. This was not the case with my parents, as is evidenced by the aforementioned "winter door policy."

But, no one was more faithful to his word than Dad. He never said a word he didn't mean. If Dad said you're going to get beat, in layman's terms that meant "you're going to get beat." I seem to have been the kind of parent who could only dole out punishment at the time of the crime. After that I would mellow out and not have the heart to follow through. Not Dad. If he came home from work and Mom had a laundry list of my bad behavior to show him and he promised I would get beat, you best believe at some point in the next twenty-four hours, it would occur.

I think this was part of Dad's strategy. He would change his clothes, eat dinner, read the paper, and watch the evening news. Meanwhile, I was as quiet as a mouse, cowering in a corner, looking over my shoulder. No matter how many times Dad did this, eventually I still become relaxed. Just when I didn't expect anything I could expect something.

Dad was like a panther in a people suit. Someone may ask, "Why didn't you just go somewhere and hide?" WRONG! I would have rather run naked through a briar patch then face my father after I tried to hide. I think the next time in my column I will recount the times that I was good and didn't risk my parent's wrath. Yea, right! As if such times actually existed.

Car rides far from safety centered

Kids today are really well protected when their families go out for an afternoon drive in the family car. There are car seats, booster seats, seat belts, shoulder harnesses, you name it! That is great as far as I am concerned.

I can remember the car seat that Mom and Dad used for us when I was a kid; it stretched from one side of the car to the other and mom and dad sat on the front one and we young'uns sat on the one in the rear. And if there were anything called seatbelts in our family car Dad would have probably cut them out to make room for another young'un. The closest thing we had to a booster seat for my little brother was when he was sitting in Mom's lap on the front seat.

Things have come a long way in 50 years and safety is now a priority in the family car. Of course car manufacturers have been able to maintain safety, but also assure luxurious features as well. Today a ride in some vehicles is more like experiencing a living room on wheels. There are fold down DVD players, satellite radio and built in soft drink coolers.

It wasn't so much about luxury when I was a kid. The family car was no more than a portable storage shed. When it was time to take a family trip Mom and Dad would take their place in the front seat and we kids would commence to crawl into the back seat like a bunch of circus monkeys. There were no restraints in the back seat either. As Dad headed down the highway the three of us would be milling around the backseat like we were visiting the mall. One of us would be in the floor, another on our knees writing our name in the window fog while the other was crammed up into the rear window area waving at passing cars.

Inevitably, one of us would ram our foot and leg up under Dad's car seat, a practice that for some reason really pushed Dad's buttons. This would cause Dad to develop a slight sense of irritation. Of course the fact that the three of us had started wrestling and rolling around the back seat and floor like Sea World dolphins did little to lower his patience threshold.

Unlike Mom, who would spend a great deal of time verbally assaulting us and telling us what she was going to do if we did not behave, Dad was more a man of less words and more action. Mom was more prone to warn us in great graphic terms about car behavior. For instance, she hated for us to put our hands out the window in the summertime while the car was moving. Instead of simply telling us not to put our hands out the window, Mom would have to tell us, "Don't put your hands out the window, a car will come by and rip your arms off." She apparently thought we had arms like an orangutan, or jungle ape because most cars were at least several feet from our car at any given time.

On the other hand, Dad wasted little time simply telling us what he was going to do when we were acting like zoo animals. If for some reason Dad was in a particularly good mood, he would give us one verbal warning to "settle down" before beginning to swing his arm behind his back, attempting to strike the one child who may be within arms reach.

Of course we were aware of this tactic and having free run of the backseat we would all cram our bodies back as far against the passenger-side corner to avoid Dad's Babe Ruth-like swing. The whole time, Dad was trying to drive with one hand and get at us with the other, and we would be trying to push each other into his field of discipline. I think one time he simply jammed on the brake and we all rolled up to the front of the car where he could beat us all at once.

Perhaps I am embellishing my recollection of these episodes. I have to believe this type of behavior never went on to any extreme because we all three knew that at some point Dad would arrive at our destination and we would have to get out of the car. At that point Dad would have bounced us all into the house like basketballs at March Madness. Oh well, despite it all, life was good!

I was certainly no sports prodigy

With spring on its way it will soon be time to start the Little League season. This is a very positive outlet for young people. I find both good and bad with the modern day philosophy of "everybody plays." It seems a well-intentioned idea. If 100 kids try out for a little league team, they will all get put somewhere. But, this was not always the case. I recall as a young boy we did not always "make the team."

As I consider my young life in Crisfield, Md., there is little that I can recall that indicates anything that stands out as great talent. I never really excelled at anything that I can remember. When it came to sports, I was well-intentioned and think there may have even been a split second in time that had me resembling a fairly good third baseman. I always wanted to play first base, but as a kid I was not tall enough to be considered, although I do recall making some decent plays at that position.

Then there are the tragedies in my sports career. In the fifth grade I tried out for Biddy Beague Basketball. Tryouts were held at the National Guard Armory. When the room cleared after tryouts, me and somebody's dog were the only two who did not make a team. My father was a commander at the National Guard, so the next day he handed me a pair of tennis shoes and told me to report for practice. I was a member of the Blue Devils basketball team. I often wondered what great benefits were bestowed upon my coach by my father for making that sacrifice. Not to say I was a bad basketball player, but I think I tended to take things to literally.

I recall one of the few times that I actually played during game time, my coach told me to "stay under the basket."

Little did I realize that he meant this to happen only while the ball was being played at that end of the court. So, as action made its way to the opposite end of the court, I could still be found standing under the basket all by myself, staring up at the rim as if I was expecting Jesus to return. I don't think the coach allowed me to play another game after that.

I think I realized how bad I must have been when one Saturday I spied my father, dressed in his National Guard fatigues heading up the steps toward the basketball court. I was so excited. I would finally have the opportunity to show Dad my moves. As he reached the top of the stairs, he took a left turn and walked into the upstairs kitchen. I viewed my father through the kitchen service window as he opened the refrigerator, took out a soda and then quickly made his way back downstairs and out of sight. Either my father was very busy that day, or he feared having to be exposed to the embarrassment of my basketball court skills, or lack thereof. Either way, it did little for my young ego.

Then, at 12 years old I tried out for Crisfield Little League Baseball. When the tryouts closed out that day, me and a kid with "coke-bottle" glasses and a wooden leg were left not chosen by a team. I think I was broken hearted that day, mainly because I knew my father held no high-ranking position with the Little League organization, so I would not be hitting the baseball diamond that year. Sadly, the league did not have today's philosophy of "every kid plays." Nope. Back when I was a youngun' you only got on a team if you were good, or is your parents happened to be politically connected or just had lots of money. There was little thought given to the building of self-esteem. Hmmm. Do I sound a little bitter?

I like the idea that competitive youth sports now make rules to help assure that kids get a chance to play on a team and get actual on the field or court play time during games. But, the truth is that those of us years ago who participated in sports try outs and did not make the cut were not destroyed and left suffering devastating blows to our self-esteem. I truly believe it helped prepare me for those guaranteed disappointments that life would hand out over the years.

I was fortunate to have had a son who was good at baseball and whose heavy hitting bat made him a desired member of Little League teams he played for. So, I would sit on the bleachers at each of his games and cheer him on. I would watch him as he ran the bases and relive all of the games of my youth that I did not play and thank the good Lord that he had not gained his athletic skills from me.

It was 'Johnny Cash hits the beach'

Some unseasonal weather has left us with temperatures as high as the upper 80s in some cases. On the heels of February weather that brought record snow falls and below zero wind chills, these temperatures can appear nothing less than hot. So, I am thinking that perhaps we may be in for a very hot summer.

I spend a lot of time in the out of doors during the summer, but I am limited to the amount of exposure I allow. I am one of the few men who finds it difficult to wear shorts during the hot, humid temperatures of summer.

I am not quite sure why I am reluctant top do so; perhaps it is a mental defect. As a child I found it somewhat less than macho to be caught wearing "short-pants" as we affectionately called them.

However, also as a child I had no choice but wear them. I guess in reality I had a choice, but running around naked did not seem like an attractive option. Of course as a young boy, I was less inhibited and could be found running around in my "underpants," as they were called or as my grandmother referred to it, "drawer-tale."

But, nonetheless, the older I got the more determined I became to avoid wearing shorts. I can recall many times going to the beach in Ocean City and my girlfriend would be lying on a towel in her bikini completely doused in suntan lotion. Next to her was me. I too had a towel, but it was covering my face. There I would lie fully clothed in a blue tank-top and pair of full length black jeans. It was "Johnny Cash goes to the beach."

I have tried to figure out my aversion to wearing shorts. Maybe it's because I am ashamed of my legs. Perhaps I will fear people will make fun of me.

People can be that way. Take my mother for instance. She and my aunt would go to the beach for two reasons – Thrasher French Fries and to sit and eat Thrasher French Fries while sitting on a bench making fun of people as they walk by.

This was a regular sport for my mother. She would get the biggest kick out of finding anyone who she thinks looked worse in a bathing suit than she did. She would love to point out the man with the hairiest back, the woman with the hairiest back and so on. I guess I have always felt for those poor creatures who garnered my mother's boardwalk attention.

My wearing shorts may very well have created another human oddity that can be made fun of from the safety of a boardwalk bench. Perhaps my hatred for shorts may also stem back to a certain defense mechanism I needed when I was young.

Wearing shorts made you an easy target for an irate mother' who was running towards you with a switch after you had just thrown your little brother head-first into a pile of fresh dog manure. It was the legs that were the target for the dreaded switch. There was no way to hide. I think my arms grew six-inches trying to cover the bare flesh on my shins and ankles. Michael Jackson had nothing on us when it came to creating moves.

I know I must have looked like the original Lord of the River Dance while Mom was wearing the bark off that switch. I think, however, that the older I get, the less I am able to deal with the hot, humid summer sun. Perhaps like many older men I know, I will suddenly care less and less about my attire.

I mean it seems to me that when some men grow older they develop an attitude that dictates comfort over social acceptance. That's why some men can be found wearing white gym socks and sandals.

Then there are the fellows who wear yellow, striped slacks that are pulled up and belted between their navel and their neck. My favorites are those men who wear Bermuda shorts with black dress shoes.

I don't know. I guess wearing shorts is not all that bad. Maybe this will be the summer that I will finally overcome my fear and start taking comfort into consideration when picking out my wardrobe. I should not allow childhood fears to cause me to have a heat stroke.

I guess I could practice by wearing shorts around the house at first. Then I may ask my mother to visit. I will make shorts a part of my normal summer attire is she doesn't take one look at me and suddenly have a craving for Thrasher's French fries.

My childhood in storage

My mother is attempting to have her basement cleaned out. This is a job that has needed to be done since before my father passed away 10 years ago. She has asked her young'uns to take a look to see if there is anything that we want before she hires someone to take it all away. I decided to do my own exploration this past weekend.

The contents of Mom's basement resemble the prop warehouse at Universal Studios. As far as the eye can see there is stuff. Getting to this stuff is a journey in itself. Cobwebs hang from the ceiling like bed sheets. By the time I walked from one end of the basement to the other I looked like I had another head of hair.

My father was a hoarder. He was notorious for hanging on to anything and everything for fear either he would need it someday, or somebody else may get it if he didn't. So, Mom's basement is full of bits and pieces of clutter, very little of which actually amounts to a complete item. Every drawer is crammed full of nuts, bolts, screws and metal objects that may have once been attached to the hull of Noah's Ark.

It was difficult for me to look through the piles of rusting metals and rotting wood and not recall how much all of this mass of nothing once meant to my father. I could see him trudging into the basement from outside hauling a handful of tractor widgets and a length of garden hose under his arm. The basement was where he would stash everything so Mom was unable to see it.

When it came to storing useless items, Dad was a Master. He could fill every available space so tight a breath of air could not pass through. Dad also had a stock answer for any of us who may ask what he planned to do with all of his hidden treasures and why he didn't get rid of them. He would always say, "It ain't eating or drinking."

Pouring through the drawers of the cabinets in the basement I was amazed at how many partial items I found. There was a hoe without a handle, a hammer handle without a hammer head, bolts without nuts, nuts without bolts, the propeller from a boat and enough rifle and pistol ammunition to sponsor Armageddon.

But, amid all the clutter were items that I remember well. Three of these items I have asked my mother to allow me to keep (in her basement of course). There is the small kitchen stove that provided heat in my childhood home in Crisfield. I remember how the base of the stove would slowly fill with oil and then Mom would drop a match inside and it would blaze. I still remember like it was yesterday how my older brother Tommy and I would stick our faces into the top of the stove and watch with amazement as Mom would drop the match and the beautiful blue flame would ignite the pool of oil.

I remember sometimes there would be too much oil and a huge flame would shoot up into the back of the chimney hole and up through the roof. Mom would rush us outside and stand us away from the house while the "flames burned down." Even today, I shudder to think how this would happen while my brother and I had our heads shoved down inside the top of the stove. The stove now sits abandoned in Mom's basement and I did not have the heart to let it go.

Another stove that sits directly next to that kitchen stove is the old-fashion wood cook stove that was used at my grandparent's house. I remember so well helping to bring in the chopped wood from outside and stacking it against the wall behind that stove. I would watch my father take an iron handle and lift the round covers that sat at each corner of the stove top. He would push the wood into the raging fire and then use the handle to arrange it so he could get the lid back on. How could I part with this piece of my childhood?

Standing stately along a sidewall is a wooden cabinet. It is plain. It has one large wooden door on the front which provides a cover for five shelves that hang on the inside. A simple lift-latch keeps the door closed. There are no fancy designs or beautiful shades of paint adorning the cabinet; just a flat white. To most people looking at the cabinet it would appear somewhat bland and lacking in formalities. But, to me it is gorgeous. It was built by a man I never met, but whose life I am very familiar with. He built all kinds of furniture. He built boats. He also built houses, stores and schools. He was my mother's father; he was my grandfather.

The cabinet sat in the kitchen of my childhood home and contained some extremely important items, including financial documents, pencils and pens and a number of other items that little hands were prohibited from touching. I remember the cabinet was so tall that I stood on tip-toes trying to reach the lift-latch so I could explore the items that were being hidden from me.

As I looked at the cabinet that has been in my mother's basement for 40 years, I realize that I now tower a good foot and a half over top of it. My mother's basement is dank. It is cold, dark and wet. The paint on the cabinet has not so much as cracked, and not one-inch of wood has deteriorated or shown any signs of weakening. That, my friend, is the mark of a great craftsman. I wish I could have inherited just a little of his carpentry talent. Instead I can barely build a fire, much less a piece of furniture.

Mom's basement is far from inviting. It is much like a room I would expect to see inhabited by bats, snakes and a lost mining crew. Ninety-nine percent of everything in the basement is trash. But, that one percent of items that represent the heart and soul of my father, grandfather and my childhood are priceless.

Whatever she had handy

The faith that young kids have is great. When you're a kid you believe that a bumblebee or a firefly can live in a jar just as long as you poke holes in the lid.

I remember every summer I would be found in the yard scanning the yellow dandelions for honey bees. It was amazing the talent I had for catching many creatures with nothing more than a jar and lid.

I could fill a jar with bees in the morning and then in the evening go out and catch fire flies or "lightening bugs" as we called them. I can still remember the many nights I would got to sleep watching the fire flies on one side of my bed as their tales lit on and off, almost in concert. On the other side of the bed I could hear the muffled buzzing of about a dozen bees.

I had to sneak the jars into my bedroom because mom would have beat me till I was a midget if she knew I had brought bees into the house. For some unknown reason she had a problem with spending all day trying to keep the summer pests outside, only to have me bus them in at night.

Of course we kids didn't make the job any easier. We were in and out of the house like air. Not that it really mattered, because I can't recall the screen on the screened-door ever being without tears big enough to stick your head through.

It was amazing. None of us kids could open the screened door using the handle. I mean, this door had a handle the size of a crowbar, but we still had to push on the screen to open the door.

After about four or five shoves, the screen would begin to tear around the edge. Within only about three to four more shoves, someone's hand would bust through. Of course it was the hand that actually broke through that got all the blame.

I remember one day my younger brother and I were arguing. We started shoving each other around and he ran outside. He stood on the other side of the screen making faces and taunting me. He put his face against the screen and having had enough, I took the book I was reading and threw it at him. Fortunately, my brother moves his face before the full collection of Aesop's Fables struck the imprint where only a few moments earlier his face had been.

Unfortunately, the book tore through the screen like a bulldog tearing through a hambone and I was suddenly looking at a screen hanging by only one corner. Now, I know my parents would understand that my brother's face-making and dancing about like a drunken sailor would be enough to cause anyone to have a sudden loss of good judgment and at the least, throw a book through the screen door. Sure they would. Now, back to reality.

My brother was pleased. As a matter of fact, he was ecstatic. He was so happy for me that he ran as fast as he could to share his joy with my mother who was hanging clothes out on the clothesline. As she had approached the house I was understandably concerned that she had for some reason, stopped long enough to pick up an old wooden shingle that blown off the roof.

Now, bear in mind that unlike my Dad, whose primary tool of discipline was his belt, my mother was a woman of great variety. She would dole out our beatings with whatever was handy. Though I was worried about the wooden shingle, I considered myself lucky that she had not reached for the clothesline prop instead.

Much to my brother's chagrin Mom was also one who cared less about who actually did the deed of destruction as she did about the fact we were both fighting with one another when the incident occurred.

My brother's leaps of joy suddenly turned into the "whupping dance" as my mother struck his bare leg with the shingle. In my mother's defense, she always had a knack for choosing lightweight, easily breakable things to beat us with, such as a yardstick.

So, like the yardstick, the shingle broke on my brother's legs and when she got around to me she was striking my arms and legs with apiece of balsa wood the size of a baseball card.

Of course both my brother and I wailed like we were being beat half to death. It was good practice because later that day my father came home and was faced with having to fix a screened door that had been torn by a flying book. I don't really recall, but I'm sure we were probably actually beat "half to death."

Matt Dillon and my father

I hear a lot about the influence that media has on society. It is true and it has been since the first stone tablet. As a youngster there is no doubt that media influenced me. I think back in the 1960s and 1970s the influence was a bit more innocent than it tends to be today. Nonetheless, I was influenced by movies and television.

I was saddened to hear on Friday about the death of actor, James Arness, who portrayed a U.S. Marshal whose office was located in Dodge City, Kansas. Outside of my father, Matt Dillon was one of the most significant role models of my youth. It may sound foolish, but you have to consider the role that James Arness played as Matt Dillon. Matt Dillon was a lawman as was my father. When Matt Dillon and Dad were working they both would come into my living room wearing a Stetson hat and brandishing a leather holster and gun around their waist.

Matt Dillon was a no-nonsense lawman. He never backed down from doing what was right, even in the face of scenarios that seemed to be against all odds. It seemed, based on the weekly television schedule at any rate, that Matt Dillon lived and breathed his job as a Marshal. There was no doubt that my father lived and breathed his job as a state policeman, county sheriff and chief of the Crisfield Police Department.

The same morals and codes of conduct that Matt Dillon subscribed to as the chief law enforcement officer in Dodge City mirrored the values that my own father possessed. It was never what Dad said as much as what he did that had the greatest influence on me as a child. We must be painfully aware that children often have the ability to tune out their parents or other authority figures when they are being given a verbal life's lesson. However, children almost always watch the behavior and attitude of the people they most admire. It is my belief that watching how my parents reacted to situations and conducted their affairs in both private and public had the greatest influence on the man I am today.

As a young boy every Monday night I would be found in front of the black and white television watching as Matt Dillon took his spot in the middle of Dodge City to face down the outlaw in a main street shootout. That was how the show started each week. I always felt comfortable that my father would have fit in perfectly having coffee in Matt Dillon's office shooting the breeze with Matt, Festus Hagin and Doc Adams.

Interestingly enough, James Arness served in the U.S. Army in World War II, seeing battle in the invasion of Anzio, Italy. He was wounded in the leg. The wound caused him to have a limp for the rest of his life. My father enlisted in the Army during World War II, but saw his combat in Korea, where he was also wounded in the leg by a bullet and took shrapnel from a hand grenade.

I have no regrets for finding a sense of moral direction in the adventures of a fictitious character from the old West. I always found Matt Dillon to simply be a character that confirmed the value system that my father strived to impart on his less than innocent, heathen young'uns. I was so influenced by the television portrayal of Marshal Matt Dillon that each year at Christmas the only thing I asked for was a new single holster gun belt and revolver.

I was always happy that John Wayne turned down the role of Matt Dillon and instead convinced his good friend James

Arness to take the role. John Wayne told Arness, who was six-foot, six-inches tall, that actors like him and Gregory Peck didn't want a "big lug like you towering over us." Instead he advised Arness to, "Make your mark in television." Good advice, I think.

I was so impressed with James Arness' portrayal of Marshal Matt Dillon that I wrote him a letter a few years ago to tell him so. I told him how much his character was like my father and watching him each week helped me as a young boy to recognize and admit how proud I was to have a father who was a lawman and more importantly someone who would never shirk from doing what was right. Arness thanked me with an autographed copy of his autobiography. The book, a U.S. Marshal badge and a portrait of James Arness as Matt Dillon are kept in a special place in my home today.

Also, in a special place in my home is a shadow box that holds my father's Maryland State Police 38-caliber revolver. The gun is held in place with two of the silver bullets from Dad's Somerset County Sheriff's gun belt, along with a uniform patch from his Chief of Police work shirt. All of these are prized reminders of two men who helped shape my moral code of conduct as a young boy growing up in Crisfield, Md.

Perhaps I grew up low on tar?

I recall as a young boy growing up in Crisfield, Md., that I was reminded of the consequences of my typical heathen behavior. My mother had threatened on numerous occasions to beat the "stuffing, fire, breath, daylight, devil" or possibly" the tar" out of me. Of all these opportunities I am still convinced that only one was actually possible. Since I still have my breath, I have to assume Mom was over-stating her intentions.

But, it is important to remember that my poor mother was only reacting to the stress of three young'uns. I was lucky she had not found the secret to beating the stuffing out of me. However, if she could have beaten the devil out of me I think I would have been so much more manageable. Mom was very good at verbalizing at great lengths before actually carrying out any type of discipline. We would hear for what seems like hours of how fed up she was with our ape-like actions. Mom was notorious about following us from room to room, yelling and graphically explaining why she was about to beat us until Jesus returned.

Dad, on the other hand, said very little before "knocking us seven ways from Sunday." Now, I am far from an engineer or philosopher, but there was something about imagining being catapulted through the air at the wrong end of Dad's hand, and passing Sunday seven different times and ways.

Dad was a man of few words and much more action. So, when he took the time to explain just how hard he was going to hit us, we listened and took it seriously. If ever there was someone who could in fact beat the fire out of me, it was Dad; even if he had to light the kindling first.

There is no question we Windsor boys feared Dad. Unlike Mom he was quick to action and allowed little time to gather between when he warned and when he struck. Dad was the kind of man who could stare us in the eye and hypnotize us into telling him the truth. It had to be hypnosis because there is no rational reason for me to tell the truth in the face of so much potential violence.

In this day and age, I am sure there are those who read this and find it grotesque that I would make light of what by virtue of my words may equate to child abuse. Well, I will say to those people that instead of "child abuse," I consider my mother and father's form of discipline to have been swift and immediate justice. I knew even while I was being dealt with by my parents that it came as the result of teaching me to be moral and responsible. I never felt I was being "beat" because my Dad had a bad day. I was in control of whether or not my father had to resort to action beyond words. I knew what was right, but often headed toward that which was wrong. That alone leaves me completely baffled to this day. Why did I so often tempt the wrath of my father when I had it within my grasp to avoid it?

Oh well, such are the follies of youth.

As much nothing as I had ever seen

Recently, I visited my mother in Marion Station. I get down there every once in a while and as soon as I step out into the yard I am overcome with a sense of nostalgia. I moved to Marion Station from Crisfield, which is about seven miles away, when I was about 13 years old. So, like Crisfield, Marion Station is also hometown to me.

As I walked through the backyard toward the field at the rear of Mom's house, I realized how many times as a teenager I most likely stood somewhere in the same vicinity wishing I was anywhere else in the world.

I remember sitting in the yard outside the house thinking about how much was happening elsewhere and how much I was missing. Now, over 35 years later, I am sitting in the same place not caring what else was going on outside of this little piece of pleasure that I was so aggressively trying to escape from. It is amazing what life's "School of Hard Knocks" can do to teach you about appreciating the little things in life.

I remember so well when we moved to Marion Station. My father and a couple of my uncles helped pack us up. We used two pickup trucks. Dad had his own process for moving. He did not suggest Mom pack things in boxes; as a matter of fact, he also suggested Mom not even be home when he started the moving job. He toted her to the new house in Marion and that is where she stayed during the ordeal. Dad simply came into the old house with his brothers and went through the rooms like Grant through Richmond.

Dad grabbed Mom's dish drainer stacked with the breakfast dished she had just washed and out the door he went with it. He came back and Dad and my uncles grabbed cupboards still loaded with dishes and pots and pan and threw them in the back of the truck. I think I recall heading down the highway with the stove in the back of the truck with biscuits still baking in the oven and a bed with my brother still sleeping in it.

Arriving at the new home in Marion Station, Dad and his brothers simply put things in place and all the dishes were in place and ready to use. It was amazing that in the process of moving only one dish was broken.

We moved on a Saturday and it was evening before we were finished. Dad knew this would be the case, so the first things that he and the brothers made sure were put together and ready for use, were all our beds.

I vividly remember the first day at our new home. I sat on the front porch and looked out over as much nothing as I had ever seen in my life. Don't get me wrong, there was a big, beautiful front yard; green and perfectly kept. Big, heavy-leaved trees blew in the wind. It was a gorgeous country setting, but loaded down with absolutely nothing to do.

Crisfield was a small town, but Marion Station made it look like New York City. As I sat on the porch and look out to the road that ran past our front yard I counted three cars every 10 minutes. Do the math, that is about one car every three minutes or so. The road was as desolate as the surface of the moon.

I would possibly have investigated some of our neighbors, if we had any within two or three miles. I left the porch and went out on the front steps hoping that I would find that I had missed something. I was right, I had missed something!

There was apparently even more nothingness that I had thought earlier.

I walked around that beautiful yard and I felt boredom literally dripping over my shoulders. I missed Crisfield and just knew all my friends were up to their earlobes in fun and adventure somewhere on Somerset Avenue.

Yet, here I was walking along a country road that seemed connected to nowhere, next to a creek so far from civilization that at any moment I expected to see Jimmy Hoffa's body float by.

It was clear to me that if I was expected to live in this scene from the outskirts of Hootersville, I would have to find something to do. I am sure I will share some of those "things" in future columns!

I thought money grew in a garden

In my young mind there was no consideration that money may be in short supply. I was rampaging along the Boardwalk in Ocean City, Md. in the summer of 1963. My brothers and I were overwhelmed with the amusement rides that flashed lights, rang bells and played the calliope music as we handed our tickets to the operator.

We would go around and around on the "Whippersnapper," the indoor Ferris Wheel and the antique merry-go-round, Waving to Mom each time we passed her standing at the fence. In our little minds this circus should never end. Unfortunately, it had to end, mainly because mom ran out of money. This was a concept that was hard for my brothers and I to grasp. The idea that money would actually stop flowing from the "Revenue River" was insane to us.

But, I can still see mom telling us that it was time to go home because she was "broke." Instead of accepting the fact that Mom had done the best she could with providing us a day of amusement, we would suddenly transform from smiley-faced, excited young boys into ungrateful, impish young'uns.

We would somehow think that by ranting and raging about how unfair it was to close the circus down, a big bird would flyover and drop $50 bills on our heads. Now that I have had the opportunity to raise my own son and on many occasions, remind him that no matter how many times he rejects the notion, money does not grow in the garden. This despite the fact that I would have certainly fertilized that proverbial garden with the load of money that he has literally flushed down the toilet.

There were three of us kids back then and going to the Boardwalk in Ocean City had to be an expensive venture for my mother. My father would provide the money, but would have no parts of actually going to the beach with us. He said it was because as a Maryland State Trooper he had to spend so much time directing traffic at the Ocean Downs harness racing tracks that he had no desire to be there when he was off-duty.

However, I think it had more to do with the fact that he had no desire trying to keep up with three rambunctious heathens like my brothers and me. Be that as it may, Mom was always ready to go to the beach with her best friend Pat Diggs. She enjoyed lying out on the beach, relaxing in the summer sun and breeze.

I think in reality it would have been more relaxing for her to have been lying out in the middle of an African antelope stampede. She could not close her eyes for worrying about one of us young'uns drifting out to Fenwick Island on one of the ocean waves, or burying our little brother, Jeff, up to his eyeballs in sand.

After Mom had dragged two webbed beach chairs, three towels, a king-sized blanket, three sand buckets and a cooler across the scorching white sands, she was able to lie back for all of about 20 minutes. That is how long it took us three kids to become bored with digging for sand crabs and jumping waves.

We would spot the Ferris wheel going around and around and all of a sudden Mom had to be hit with a nonstop barrage of "When can we go up on the Boardwalk?" That went on until Mom realized she either had to get up and move or she may be faced with criminal child abuse charges. Looking back, I know my brothers and I did little to prevent my mother from being able to correlate relaxation with any of her memories associated with the day at the beach with her kids.

The green, green grass of home

Well, it's that time of year again. It's a summer time. You've got to love it. Wrong.

I'm not saying that summer is no fun at all. It can be; but the question is for whom? Maybe for the hordes of young people who are out of school, but certainly not for the working man and woman. The way I see it, when it's cold you can always bundle up. There's no end to the coats, sweaters, gloves and scarves you can pile on. But, when it's hot you can only get so naked.

It's not bad enough that I have to come home from work each day to face another hot, humid evening at home. I don't even get to the front door before I am faced with the harsh reality that my yard has become some type of wildlife sanctuary. I've never seen anything to match the success of growing grass and weeds. Recently, my lawn was damaged during an emergency water main replacement on Delaware and Pennsylvania avenues. The contractor and the city were very responsive, clearing the yard, putting on new topsoil and planting grass.

My excitement about this project was not completely related to the fact that I was getting a newly planted lawn. It was the fact that a huge chunk of my yard was now topsoil and I would not have to cut grass in that area. Joy! I could bask in the fact that I would only be cutting grass on a little more than half my yard. Certainly it would be fall before that grass would be tall enough to cut. Wrong.

About a week after the grass had been planted the blades began to push their pointed little heads up through the topsoil. Within a week and a half, I actually saw clumps of grass. I looked outside this morning and I could swear that was corn growing out there. This is not normal grass. It is some type of mutant, hybrid creation. I feel like I will come home today and find monkeys swinging from the tops of this grass. I guess I must have a bad attitude. I should see my grass as something beautiful; my lawn as a precious possession. But, I'm so busy. I work two jobs and by the time I get out to mow the lawn, I am walking behind the lawnmower with a 12-gauge shotgun, fearing that at any moment a wild boar or some other beast will leap up from under the brush.

I cut the lawn a few weeks ago and when I finished I found a bicycle, shopping cart, two sets of golf clubs and a homeless man. I may be exaggerating, but this helps me to make light of a chore that I so wholeheartedly dislike. Oh well, it's only a few months and I'll finally get some rest, just in time to shovel some snow.

I love the smell of coffee

There is something that is down-home comfortable about the smell of freshly brewed coffee. It has an odor that refreshes me just like the smell of my grandfather's cigar used to do when I was a kid. As much as I love to smell coffee, I have no desire to drink it.

I think I enjoy the smell so much because it reminds me of my youth. However, I think that with the exception of me, everyone in my family loves coffee. So why don't I drink coffee like my parents and my brothers? Because my father made sure that I would not be a coffee drinker way back when I was four-years old. I recall sitting at the kitchen table watching my father eat breakfast. He would always have his eggs cooked soft. He would burst the yellow of the egg and stir it up into an almost artistic creation. He would then say, "Francis (that's my mother) where's the mustard?" He would take a fork and spread mustard all over his eggs. Next, he would slice sharp cheese from a block and then drop the slices into his hot, steaming coffee.

After he had gotten my mother to deliver his toast, my father would dip his fork into the coffee and come out with a wet, brownish-yellow muddle of cheese that he would put on his toast; instant toasted cheese sandwich. Then he would take his coffee pour it into a saucer, so as to cool it, and then drink the coffee from out of the saucer. If there's one thing I was sure of it was my father's love for his coffee.

I was in awe of his early morning ritual. My father was a legend in my young eyes and I had emulated every single step of his breakfast tradition. I would burst the yellow in my egg and smear mustard all over the sticky, yellow pile in my plate. But, I was too young to drink coffee. I don't really know at what age it became legal for you to drink coffee, but at four years of age, I had not reached that point. My father sensed my desire to be just like him, so he figured a way to both maintain this endearment and to keep me from drinking coffee.

As I begged and pleaded for Dad to give me some of his coffee, he continued to drink and tell me that I didn't need it. It's a funny thing about parents, they never feel you can have something simply because you want it; it has to be something you need before you can have it.

As I begged for the coffee, which I was sure would cause me to grow another six inches and gain 14 years on my age age, my father looked at me and said, "All right, you can drink the rest of mine."

This was incredible! No only was my father, the human rock, going to allow me to drink coffee, but he was going to allow me to do it from his own cup. This, my friends, was a moment.

Little did I realize this was all part of the ruse. This was the beginning of the end for me and my short-lived love for coffee. My father had drank all but a small amount of his coffee. All that was left was an ounce of liquid and two pounds of coffee grounds, lying beneath the coffee.

I took a big swallow and almost immediately gained the sensation that must come when you eat a cigar. As I tried to push the tiny, granular coffee grounds off my tongue, it was not unlike the day I fell off the monkey bars and sucked 10-pounds of playground sand into my mouth. That was it! No more! From that moment on I have never had any desire to drink coffee.

As usual, my father had been successful in his ploy. He kept his young son from being swept into the hazards and debauchery of coffee addiction. I thank him today.

This same type of psychological training also kept me from ever desiring the taste of a beer. I recall at the age of five, I was playing outside and a group of guys in a blue, 1961 convertible, threw a can of beer out of the car. I watched the red can roll across the highway and it came to rest against the curb by my house. I looked as the yellow, foaming liquid came pouring out of the small opening in top of the can.

I couldn't resist. I had to have my first taste of the forbidden. I picked up the can, placed it to my lips and took a big swallow. Yuck! Horrors! It was hot beer and tasted terrible. To this day I have never desired a beer. But, sometimes I find myself still hoping that that was truly beer that was inside that can that was thrown from the car.

Snakes can be a hoot

I was watching a National Geographic show the other night. It was about a guy who travels around the world gathering animal tissue samples and venom to be used in scientific projects to create cures for different illnesses. I become totally mesmerized when I watch these adventurists handle venomous snakes.

I have always wondered about the common snake and how it raises a certain degree of fear in people. People are scared to death about the prospects of a snake in their path, yet will break their necks to see one on television or at the zoo.

This is the way it is with my mother. She is scared to death anytime she hears the word "snake," yet she would knock you down to see one on television. My mother's great fear of snakes presented a level of joy to my father whose sadistic sense of humor went into play anytime he saw a snake crawl across the years.

It was not important that the snake be alive. It could be a dead snake and still create the same sense of fear. I can recall one summer afternoon at my grandmother's house in Marion Station. We would always gather as a family and have Sunday dinner at grandmother's farm.

My father had been in the chicken house houses checking on a new bath of hens that had recently been purchased, when from behind a corn sheller a big, black sane slithered by. Now, it would have been simple to have ignored the scaled creature, but because of the damage the black snake can create in a chicken house, Dad went hunting.

It was an amazing thing to watch my father catch a snake. He would run up on the beast and with a quick snatch, grab the snake by the neck. Like a bullwhip, he would snap the snake's neck within seconds. Now, I'm sure this may not set well with animal rights activists, but to a farmer a snake represents dead chickens and sucked up eggs.

Now, Dad could have just thrown the dead snake carcass out in the field for the buzzards, but that would have lacked the fun of a good snake scare. I can still see Dad heading up the path from the chicken house to the farm house, the motionless snake wrapped around his arm and held secretly behind his back. As he entered the kitchen, my mother sat talking with my grandmother and some of my aunts and uncles. It was actually quite sad, because I knew my mother was oblivious to the sudden horror that was about to be thrust upon her.

Suddenly, seeing Dad come across the floor out of the corner of her eye, Mom knew something was out of character. Why would he have that unnatural smirk on his face? Why was he walking with his arm behind his back? It seemed that almost instinctively, my mother" 'suddenly diagnosed the situation: SNAKE!

As my mother jumped from her chair and screamed, my father knew there was no holding back. He thrust the lifeless snake out from behind his back and went into pursuit. Now, the snake was dead, but Mom did not know this. In her mind's eye, Dad was chasing her through the house with the Loch Ness Monster attached to his arm.

Dad was in his ultimate glory. Not only was he scaring the beejeebers out of my mother, but he had two of my aunts racing through the house like apes in a Tarzan movie. All three of the petrified women headed for the bathroom. They slammed the door shut and I am told, leaped on the bathtub.

Now, to most people with an average sense of humor, this would have been enough pleasure. Knowing these women were lined up along the edge of the bathtub like the "See, Hear and Speak No Evil" monkeys would have been adequate satisfaction. But, we are talking about my father. There was about an inch of space between the floor and the bottom of the bathroom door. My dad thrust his arm, and the better part of the first four feet of the black snake, up under the door. Like banshees, the women screamed and scurried into the bathtub, almost strangling each other with the shower curtain. The furor did not cease until the grand matriarch of the Windsor clan, my grandmother, came on the scene. Her warning "Mungst you stop that foolishness," brought Dad's fun to a halt.

Order was restored to the house and my mother was able to breathe again. However, even after discovering that the snake was dead, she was unable to find the humor in this episode. That poor old snake never knew how much pleasure he brought to that Sunday dinner.

There was a limit, believe me

Sometimes when I am in stores or restaurants I watch and listen in amazement when children confront their parents and chastise them for one issue or another. It seems less than unusual for children to criticize their parents and challenge them head-on when they have somehow not fulfilled the child's wishes. I find this amazing because I suddenly begin to think what would have happened if I had somehow mustered up enough ill-conceived courage to confront my father in this manner.

Make no mistake I was prone to making ill-informed decisions as a child when it came to testing my Dad's patience. But, I think as ignorant and heathen as I was, I even knew some sense of limits as it pertained to preserving my life and safety around my father. I recall many of those instances did not end well – for me anyway.

There he was; his eyes squinted and focused on me as close as ugly on an ape. I didn't know whether to run or dig a hole. Anytime I was faced head-on with Dad's wrath I began to think very quickly of the afterlife.

I had dared to talk back to my father. There were a list of things that created frustration in Dad, but being disrespectful was at the top. More than being at the top of the list, disrespect was in a category of its own. It was suffice to say that this warranted the full brunt of Dad's disciplinary force.

I often found myself thanking Jesus that my Dad did not drink. I could only imagine how dangerous life could be for me when you cross a drunken army vet with a hard-headed teenage heathen. I can only remember that I threatened to leave home at the age of 16 because of Dad's strict rules. I think he was on his way to pack my bags and call me a cab when I made the fatal mistake of telling him I was sick of having such stupid rules to follow.

It was like watching Lon Chaney, Jr. turn into the Wolfman. Dad was on me thicker than hair on Bigfoot. He was in my face so close I could see the back of his head. It was difficult for me to forecast when he may start the whooping session and which hand or foot may come first.

You would think I may have figured out just how far to push my father before I could count on him to push back. My older brother, Tommy, he could stay within the limits of Dad's furor. He knew just how far to go before retracting and leaving well enough alone; but, not me. For some reason, I had the terrible habit of finding it necessary to get the last word in.

There was never any doubt in my mind that being disrespectful to Dad would result in the potential of me being beat like a dirty rug, but never deterred me from doing it. I cannot to this day understand this rationale. There is no doubt in my mind that I respected my Dad greatly and at the same time feared him.

My father lived by example. He always presented himself in a way that we young'uns could watch and learn the traits of honesty, compassion and loyalty during a simple trip to town with Dad.

People respected my father and he was always greeted with friendly waves and joking conversations. It seemed like everybody knew my father. No matter where we went scores of people made it a point to stop and talk with him and share personal stories.

How is it that a man who draws this much appreciation and respect from throughout several communities could turn into a belt-wielding mad man. The reason was simple – heathen young'uns.

The fact is here was a hard working, honest, God-fearing country man who paid his bills and taxes and took care of his family. Yet, he was cursed with a big-headed, rebellious, son who thought he knew it all.

Here is a fact to consider. At the age of 16, I was challenging the limits of my father's patience and making life harder on him and me. I was moaning about going to school and having a curfew; complaining about not being able to be treated as an adult.

However, at the age of 16, my father was lying about his age to get into the Army. He spent months in basic training at Fort Dix and then spent his 17th birthday in the foxholes and bitter cold weather of Korea. Before he got out of his predicament and returned home, he was a Sergeant in charge of a squad that was literally wiped out during combat. He returned home with grenade shrapnel and a large bullet hole in his leg.

For some tragic reason, that somehow means so much more to me today than it did when I was 16. But, in the end, Dad prevailed. Everything that I have accomplished today and whatever I am that is good in a man, I owe to my father. Thanks, Dad!

Landscaping was not in my future

As I gaze outside my dining room window I see that the gray, gloomy sky has been joined by a wet, heavy mixture of cold rain and most recently, a sleet combination. This type of day's weather can easily lead to dreams of summer time and a warmer environment. Although, summer time does brings with it things such miseries as yard work and sweat.

This causes me to recall the days when as a young boy I was expected to take care of cutting the grass and trimming the hedges. I find it amazing that my father actually trusted me with a power tool such as a lawn mower and those hedge cutting implements that to me resembled a huge pair of scissors.

I hated cutting grass. I still do. I have had someone cut my grass for me for a number of years. I suppose in truth it is because I am a master procrastinator. Procrastination is something that does not fit well with the job of cutting grass. The problem with me cutting my grass is that I have a bad habit of not getting around to it on a routine basis. I procrastinate until I need a bush hog to get to the front door. I have often found myself cutting the yard in grass so tall I would not have been surprised if a herd of elk charged out or I stumbled over Jimmy Hoffa's body.

Nonetheless, I need to develop a more consistent attention to my lawn. When I was a young boy and Dad would ask me to cut the grass I would put it off until the moon was coming up, usually getting about a half the job done before it got as dark as outer space.

I also had a bad habit of rushing through the job. I would be tearing through the yard like Grant going through Richmond. Dad would always tell me that I had to comb through the yard before starting the lawn mower in order to pick up loose rocks and other debris that could tear up the blade and create a projectile that would shoot out from under the grass cutter.

Of course Dad's instructions fell on deaf ears. Actually they fell on perfectly working ears. Unfortunately, the ears were attached to my head, which was at most times nothing more than a hat rack and a place to grow hair. I would start up the grass cutter, which in itself was a job. You would have to pull the starter rope until your arm was stretched so far your knuckles dragged the ground when you walked. Usually, I would yank and pull until Dad felt sorry for me and came out and pull started the engine. For him this was no more than two pulls.

So, once the grass cutter was started I would head out. I would race around the yard, stones and broken glass flying like it was the storming of the beach at Iwo Jima. I remember seeing newspapers, paper cups, or other such items lying in plain view. Rather than take the time to stop and pick this debris up, I would head for it with a vengeance. The first passing would send the paper flying out from under the grass cutter in eight different directions. I would then realize that this looked like crap on a fresh cut lawn, so I would do what any normal, 12-year-old boy would do. I ran over it again.

I would run over the pieces of paper until they resembled confetti at a Macy's Day Parade. Somehow, in my weak state of mind, I thought having tiny pieces of multi-colored paper strewn throughout your lawn, had an appeal. I suppose in a sort of redneck, moron-centered way, it was appealing. My grass cutting skills left a lot to be desired, but in the long run, my skills did result in a positive outcome. After a time or two of experiencing my grass cutting techniques it was few and far between in terms of the times Dad would call on me to cut the grass.

Memories carved in a bed

For the past couple of weeks I have been cleaning out my attic. I built an upstairs room a few years ago to serve as a bedroom for my son. I spent several thousand dollars fixing it up as his "man cave" and two months later he moved out and got married. Like all rooms that are not lived in this became a storage hole.

Everything that came to the house and could not fit in somewhere downstairs would be sent to the attic. Every piece of junk that I found some reason not to throw away was conveniently stored in the upstairs attic. I now want to use this as an office and I had to face the music and start the clean up project, hence the 25-cubic yard roll-off dumpster in my backyard.

As I went through the attic throwing piles and piles of my history out the attic door, I saw an old familiar friend lying under several sheets of plywood and a broken television. It was the bed from my childhood home in Crisfield.

I couldn't believe it. This was the bed I started sleeping in just after the crib. At age 4, I first shared it with my older brother and then it eventually became the bed I alone slept in until I married at age 18 and left home. It is like an old friend.

I now have my new (old) bed and was amazed to find that on the headboard are the carvings I made, declaring my undying love for Cheryl Marshall, a young lady whom I was smitten with in the eighth, ninth, and tenth grades. I'm not sure what her feelings were for me, but I think it was possible she may have actually known my last name. I had a propensity for liking girls who thought of me much like a pimple; they would rather not have one, but it still comes around.

Nonetheless, the carvings, featuring huge hearts with our names inside, remain as a testament to my half of the love affair. There are also small holes in the headboard ,that were made by darts, I can still see my younger brother flaying to and fro as the he skillfully dodged the flying darts I chucked at his head because he dared to lie in my bed reading one of my Superman comics.

Another neat feature on my childhood bed are the four wooden coconuts that sit perched on the posts at the corners of the bed frame. These would screw off and were wonderful projectiles to use when your brothers invaded your space. Mom quickly grew tired of picking them up off the floor so she Super-Glued™ them tightly in place.

As I moved the bed across the attic floor I recalled each childhood memory, like the times my brother and I would lie in bed exchanging stories and tickling each other to see who would laugh the hardest. Of course, for some strange reason, my parents felt we should be lying quietly in bed. No way, it was party time. My father seemed to have the biggest problem with this arrangement. His verbal warnings, which seemed to run in sync with the timing of television commercials, could be heard from the living room doorway at the base of the stairs.

First, he would say, "All right up there, knock it off." Then a few minutes later he would say, "You heard what I said. Shut it up or I'm coming up there." We knew we were safe as long as we could hear Dad's warnings. It was when his warnings stopped and were replaced by silence that was frightening. He moved like a Ninja in the night. I cannot ever recall being prepared for Dad's assaults. After about two or three warnings he would spring into action like a jungle soldier.

He would somehow make his way up the squeaky, old stairs without a sound. It was only when his form could be made out in the moonlight, hovering over us like Bigfoot with a belt, that we knew we were doomed. No time to prepare. My brother and I would almost beat each other to death trying to dodge the motions of Dad's belt. My brother and I would be grabbing for the same pillow, trying to cover as much of our body as possible. It was utter mayhem.

The rest of the night would be spent listening to each other whimpering and stifling our crying until it sounded like two plungers clearing out a clogged drain, so as not to upset Dad again. Yes, that bed brings back some remarkable memories.

Halloween, the height of autumn

There was something about the chill of autumn that did not set well with me when I was growing up. As an adult, October is by far my favorite month of the year. It is the crisp autumn air and the changing of the leaves that seems to denote some type of magic in the air. It is chilly, but not cold; warm at times, but not hot. It is just perfect.

However, as a young boy autumn signaled the end of outside weather as we had come to know it. It meant the days were getting shorter and the air colder as night fell. It was too far from Christmas and gave me little to look forward to in an immediate sense. And even though I had a love for the first week or so of school because I could show off my new back-to-school wardrobe and reunite with some old friends, by October I was tired of school. So, October did not necessarily represent my favorite time of the year.

As a youngster I had to improvise and find something to take my mind off the fact that there would be three months to Christmas and at least a month until the Sears "Wish Book" came out. So, I set my sights on Halloween. I know that a lot of people tend to see Halloween as a very negative and almost sacrilegious holiday, but to a child it means nothing except trick-or-treat and bags full of candy. It means dressing up and looking silly or scary and getting bags full of candy. Walking for what seems like miles just to get bags full of candy. Do you sense a common denominator here?

The only negative to me was the fact that Halloween was only one night. It is not like Christmas where even though it is just one day, actually one morning, that bring so much excitement, Halloween did not come with a week's vacation from school. Once we woke up the day after Halloween, we were back in school. However, there was something exciting about sharing stories with your friends the weeks and days before Halloween about who "you are going to be" for Halloween. There were the traditional witches, devils, Batman and Superman.

I of course, had no choice but to chime in about what my plans were. But, I knew in the scheme of things, it would ultimately be up to my mother to decide what my costume would be. The fact is I cannot ever recall wearing a costume for Halloween. I wore a mask. That's right. I was many different characters for Halloween during my childhood. I was Superman, Batman, the devil and even once I was Casper the Friendly Ghost. All of these characters had one thing in common, they dressed like Tony Windsor

Mom would proudly come home with a mask for me and my brother," Tommy. We could choose what we wanted to be, however, the only consideration was whether the mask I chose was big enough to fit over my unusually large head. You would think it would be simple to just take an old sheet and cut a hole in it and drape it over my body to make the perfect Casper the ghost costume. The only thing is, though there were a few old sheets in my house they were all covering a few old beds. I would just as soon have asked Mom to cut a hole in the living room curtains as I would have asked to cut holes in one of her bed sheets. I knew that was out of the question.

So, off I went, grinning, white plastic Casper face and all. Friends would come by dressed as witches with black pointy hats and black nylons, and ghosts peering from under long, white, flowing sheets. I would be walking down the sidewalk with my older brother, both of us wearing our 10-

cent store mask, dressed in work shoes and a pair of jeans. We looked like we were more likely to be robbing a convenience store than going trick-or-treating.

But, as Mom would say when we complained about the lack of a full-body costume, "How about you don't go at all?" So, I suppose given that option, we were very satisfied with our attire.

A bunch of inconsiderate oafs

My maternal grandmother was nothing less than a saint. I say that without reserve because many people called her, "St. Elizabeth." She was crippled at a very young age by rheumatoid arthritis, which destroyed every joint in her body.

As a young boy I helped my grandmother get in and out of the bed and wheeled her around the house. She spent most of the day seated in a chair in the living room near the television set. Though she was constantly racked with pain she never uttered a single complaint. The only thing I think I can ever remember her asking for was for me to read the Crisfield Times newspaper to her each week so that she would know who had died and what was on sale at the A&P store.

But, I'm sure the young heathen I was, I probably complained about any little thing this loving lady asked for that didn't fit into my planned daily schedule. One event sticks out in my mind when my entire family may have slighted this wonderful soul.

I was about 15 years old, living in Marion Station, Md., with my family. We had recently moved from Crisfield to Marion Station where my father was originally from. It is only about seven miles up the road from Crisfield, so it wasn't that significant of a move.

As a youngster I was prone to have very vivid, active nightmares. These dramas would cause me to often get up out of bed and act out my dreams. On this one night I "awoke" in the wee hours of the morning, about 2 a.m., as I recall, to the nightmare that the house was on fire. I could see the flames leaping out of the windows of my brother's bedroom. Now, understand, even though this was a dream it was very real to me at that moment.

I charged out of the bedroom and began pounding on the bedroom doors of my two brothers who slept upstairs where my bedroom was located. I screamed at the top my lungs, "The house is on fire! Get up! Get out!" I then went full speed down the stairs screaming the whole way down. "The house is on fire, get out!"

I did this all the way into the living room where I was met by my frantic mother and father. I could not stop yelling that the house was on fire. Within a couple minutes, Dad, who was very aware of my propensity for sleepwalking and nightmares, was able to ascertain that I was once again dreaming. He figured this out when I told him that I saw the flames leaping from one side of the house, while looking out the window on the other side of the house. After a few minutes of expressing relief, we all headed back to a respective bedrooms and an opportunity finish out the night sleep.

The next morning my mother went into my grandmother's bedroom to take her a cup of coffee. My bedridden grandmother, never missing a beat, asked my mother if she was finally coming to rescue her from the fire.

My grandmother had heard all the commotion and my screams that the house was on fire. She waited for someone to come to the door and pull her out of the flames. However, she never heard another thing. I suppose the next sounds she expected to hear were the firemen bursting through her bedroom windows with fire axes.

It seems funny, but in reality my grandmother went through a few anxious moments before she realize that it must have all been a terrible mistake. I can't imagine that we would not have realized that this poor, crippled woman was lying in the back bedroom hearing all the horrific news, only to have us return to bed and leave her to know no difference. My God, we were a bunch of inconsiderate oafs.

My grandmother, "Saint Elizabeth," and me
not long before she died in 1981.

Love wrapped in a broken body

I heard someone say recently that heroes are a thing of the past. Kids today seem more prone to look up to a rock or rap singer as someone who truly demonstrates character they feel worth emulating. I thought about that and tried to give serious thought to what a "hero" actually is.

I guess my definition of a hero is someone who has virtues which cause you to want to be like them. It didn't take me long to realize that I was blessed with a unique "hero," someone whom I have spent most of my adult life wishing I could be like. My hero came in the form of a woman who barely weighed 100 pounds, yet had the strength to face life circumstances that even today cause me to remain in awe. I am talking about my grandmother and she was born in the little seafood community of Crisfield, Maryland. Her name was Elizabeth Thomas, and she was married by the time she was 13. At the age of 14, she felt the first pangs of rheumatoid arthritis, a disease that would take a severe toll on her before it finally led to her death in 1982.

Her mother also had this dreaded disease, so my grandmother, out of necessity, virtually raised her younger brothers. Even though she was married at the tender age of 13, she was far older than years could ever reveal.

Her husband died before my parents were married and when they did get married they moved in with my grandmother. My earliest recollections of my grandmother are seeing her sitting in the living room chair reading the newspaper. By the time I reached the age of four or five, she lost the use of her legs altogether and was confined to a wheelchair.

Slowly, the arthritis began to creep through her body, exploding each joint as it went. She could no longer walk, but that didn't stop her from demanding her independence. I can still see her each morning wheeling up to the bed and after pulling the bed coverings up, use the yardstick to flatten and straighten the covers until the bed was immaculate.

As the arthritis began to attack her knuckles and wrists, she was still insistent on writing letters with a fountain pen she kept in a bedroom bureau. Arthritis began to transform her loving hands into jointless extremities that could no longer grip a pen or hold a phone. Though frustrated, she still fought to claim victory over this disease and insisted on doing things herself. It would seem that circumstances could get no worse for this little woman, but that unfortunately proved untrue. Ulcers had formed behind her eyes and before long they burst and stole her last great love, her eyesight. Now crippled and blind, my grandmother fell into a season of depression. But, amazingly enough, without a hint of reasoning, she suddenly burst back into life as though she had just needed time to gather her thoughts.

I was fortunate to have been one of the grandchildren that she depended on to help her get ready in the morning and also help her to bed at night. Each morning she was able to move her body out of the bed and carried it over to the waiting wheelchair; actions that represented some of the last movements she could do completely on her own.

I can remember getting her hot water for her wash basin in the bedroom and leaving the room while she would wash. Then my mother would help my grandmother into her dress and brush her hair. She had an almost constant happy disposition and never can I recall her uttering any words of complaints or self-pity.

One night I wheeled her into her bedroom and after she pulled her small body from the chair into the bed, I helped her with her medication and then as usual, knelt down at her bedside and said my prayers. Little were we to know what blow was to be dealt to this woman who every day faced her disability with the courage and love of a Saint.

For some unknown reason, the next morning as she made the move from the bed to her wheelchair, the ceiling caved in and my grandmother was thrown to the floor and covered in plaster. This freak accident would now rob her of her last semblance of independence and from that point on she had to be lifted into, and out of, the bed. By now it would be easy to understand if she were to lapse into depression and cursed the God that she so loved; but this was not the case. She never changed her attitude and remained the jovial, goodhearted, person everyone loved. She never once complained about the accident and even said she believed there was a reason why she was living a life plagued with pain. I couldn't understand it myself, but being young, I guess I didn't concern myself with seeking discernment.

When I married at age of 18, I can remember my grandmother sharing these words with me, "Honey, you take good care of her. Love her and always be good to her. I want you to be happy." At that moment I realized that I was leaving not only my family, but a woman who was more than my grandmother, she was my friend. She understood me even when I was wrong. I suddenly felt I had wasted my whole life by not paying attention to what this woman was to me.

In a few years, wracked with constant pain, my grandmother somehow became addicted to the medication that she needed to help her sleep and relax her nerves. The problem became so bad that my mother and father were forced to place her in "Deer's Head Center," in Salisbury; a move that literally broke my parents' hearts. Deer's Head was where my grandmother's mother had spent her last years of life, and it was to be where my grandmother would spend the last three years of her life.

When she entered the hospital she was addicted to drugs and had developed a personality that was not her own. Totally different and void of the loving disposition she had always displayed, my grandmother now wanted to die. But I know now that it was not God's plan to have this courageous Saint leave this world in this way.

We watched as this 65-year-old woman went through the pains of drug withdrawal, accompanied by the bitter symptoms of arthritis, which never let up for a second. But, her inner strength won and within a matter of months my grandmother was back to the loving, wonderful person everyone was used to. In the last couple of years of her life, she, accompanied by my mother, was able to take trips with the Deer's Head staff to Ocean City, Md., and be involved in various picnics and other social events.

She loved to go to the Deer's Head Center's church services and give her testimony; a testimony that so moved the people who heard it that they taped it and took it back to their own church services. Lying in the bed that was rolled down to the services, she would raise her hand and begin to speak saying, "I want to thank God for being so wonderful to me. He has given me children and grandchildren that love me and care about me. I'm so lucky."

It amazes me that she could consider herself lucky after living a life plagued with pain and misery. Now I can look back and realize that my grandmother had found the true meaning of happiness. She had the courage to look past the physical and focus instead on what really brought peace and happiness, and that was love. Could I ever consider the life that my grandmother lived to be in any way worth the sacrifices she had endured?

Well, I know she no longer bears those pains and was able to sustain the brief momentary afflictions of this world. I know my grandmother touched many lives and provided an inspiration to many people who were going through hard times. Perhaps that was to be her lot in life; to serve as an inspiration. Anytime I find myself complaining about how bad things are for me or how depressed I am, I remember my grandmother, and suddenly my problems don't seem all that bad. Thanks, Grandmom.

Waiting for the fire to burn down

Whenever there are inclement weather conditions such as snow and ice, most parents are glued to the television or surfing the Internet the first thing in the morning to see if there are school cancellations or delays. I was trying to recall how my mother learned whether there were school cancellations or delays when I was growing up. I do recall that often Mom herself would make the call.

I can remember when Mom, wrapped in a blanket, would come to the bedroom door to let us know we were not going to school. But, it was not always because there was snow, ice or flooding conditions on the road; sometimes it was simply because it was too cold to move around the house. Our household heating system ran on a wing and a prayer, and if the pilot light went out on the living room or kitchen stove, it was more than a notion to get it back on again. We had more holes and openings in the walls of our house than a screened door. It was cold enough to hang meat in the hallways and we had enough snow on the floor by the windows to build a snowman.

Mom seems to think that school was never closed, no matter how cold it was or how much snow was on the ground. I think she is right because I remember hiking to school with snow up to my knees. I would be wearing those rubber boots that allowed snow to run down inside. By the time I got to school, I had a boot full of icy cold water and toes that felt like they were about to break off. I knew it was cold when Mom walked around the house wrapped in a blanket like Sacajawea. When she talked the steam from her breath looked like she was smoking a cigar. Nine times out of ten, we would have no running water because the pipes would freeze. It would get so cold in my grandmother's room her false teeth would freeze while soaking in the bowl.

In my mind's eye I can still see Mom trying to re-light the small oil stove in the kitchen. She would turn the oil on and it would drain down and make a liquid trail into the base of the stove. Once oil was visible, Mom would throw a lit match down on top of it.

My older brother, Tommy, and I would stand on a box and stick our heads down inside the mouth of the stove to watch as the match met the oil and started a blazing ring of fire at the bottom of the stove. We could not have been anymore entertained if we were watching a three-headed monkey juggle a dozen bananas. There was no legitimate reason why that stove did not flare up and burn us bald, or worse. But I guess folks were not as fire prevention savvy in those days.

Sometimes oil would race into the base of the stove too fast and thick. When Mom threw the match down it would flare up like the flames of hell. That was when Mom would grab us and pull us outside to "wait for the fire to burn down some." This would involve us standing outside, hovering together like three homeless people and watching flames shoot out of the top of the chimney. Luckily, each time the fire actually did burn down some, and we could go back into the house.

Our home on Richardson Avenue in Crisfield was a tinderbox sitting on a foundation. I find it hard to imagine why it did not go up in flames on several occasions. I guess I should simply be appreciative that it didn't.

In the belly of the oil barge

I suppose the soaring gas prices can be blamed on the price of a barrel of oil. I traveled to Virginia over the weekend and as I passed through three states, I saw pump prices that seemed to change as I was pumping gas. There's little to smile about when I see the tragically high prices, especially when I make a long trip.

However, thinking about the price of oil did cause me to recollect a totally non-related memory of my youth that led to a chuckle. In the summer of 1975, I had just graduated from Crisfield High School. Since I spent my school years so wisely, and prepared so well for my future as an adult, I found myself standing in line at the boat docks in competition for a job as a scrub man on an oil barge. Now, I would venture to say that there are few jobs more demeaning and rigorous than this job. If you're not familiar, let me give you an idea of what the duties entail.

An oil barge is huge. It is like a submarine that stays above the water. Inside is just what you would expect to find in an oil barge - oil. The barges would dock after having unloaded the oil and wait on a thorough cleaning before heading back for reloading. As a scrub man, my job, along with about a dozen other highly qualified, well-educated professionals, was to climb down inside the belly of the vessel and clean it.

There are several components of this job that make it apprehensible. First of all, the deck of the barges is a flat surface void of anything but steel. On this flat surface are strategically placed doors that lift to reveal a hole and a steel ladder. As you peer down into the open hole, you see absolutely nothing, just a hole that is as black and bleak as outer space, void of the planets and stars. The smell of raw fuel hits you immediately, but there is no turning back. I noticed that leading down into the hole was a rope. I was handed a metal dustpan and ordered down the ladder. As I made my way down into the deep dark abyss, I could hear the scraping of metal on metal.

Inside the hull I now stood flat on the bottom surface of the barge. The only light came from the hole above me. All across the bottom floor of the barge other guys, most of which I remembered as classmates in younger years, before they dropped out of school or went to prison. I was the only scrub man inside the barge with a high school diploma. I quickly realized this provided me no upper hand in the deal, as someone prodded me and told me to "get to work."

Let me give you an idea of what "get to work" entails. My job required that I kneel down with dustpan in hand and scrape the oil off the floor of the barge. I would then dump the oil into a bucket that was attached to a rope. Once full, I would yank on the rope and the bucket would be lifted up through the hole by someone on deck.

We worked in two-man crews and could only stay inside the barge for 10 to 15 minutes at a time. The fuel odor was overwhelming and eventually caused lightheadedness and who knows what else. So, we would rotate with the bucket lifters every so many minutes.

I was assigned my duties with a friend, Ron S., who had both dropped out of high school two years earlier and also just got out of jail three days before taking this job. He was quick to point out that I had spent two extra years of school only to wind up with the same job he had. There was no question I was sharing the belly of an old barge with some pretty tough characters. I quickly learned this at the moment

Ron put down his dustpan, leaned back on the ladder, and lit a cigarette. Ordinarily this would have created no alarm. However, surrounded by several hundred gallons of flammable fuel incited an immediate reaction. I went up the ladder like a squirrel on meth.

At the top of the barge I handed the supervisor my dustpan and hardhat and offered no notice prior to escaping the old barge. As for those who may look down on such job ethics. I do not consider myself a quitter; I think of myself more as a survivor.

It doesn't take alot to freak me out

I seem to have spent most of last week being freaked out in some manner or another. I decided to get my van washed after the slight snow we had a while back, so off to the car wash I went. I pride myself on being able to handle most situations involving technology, not because I'm advanced in the area of technology, but because I have just been lucky.

On this particular day there was an unusually long line at the car wash, but given that my van looked like it was growing hair, I decided to wait it out. One by one the vehicles entered the car wash and one by one they came out the other end. This was a different carwash than the one I have previously used. I wanted to see if this car wash could clean my car any better than my old standby. There were a couple of things that I began to get paranoid about as I approached the car wash station. One was whether the bills were going to go easily into the money slot. I hate it when those slots spew the money back out, because you have to stick your arm out the window and struggle with the moneybox like a one armed man beating a snake with a hoe. There is never enough room to open the door and try to attack it from more convenient angle. Meanwhile people are behind you, getting angrier by the minute.

Needless to say, I was elated when the money machine sucked my bills in like an Oreck vacuum cleaner on a bowling ball. A very good thing too, because the line had become excessively long behind me. The doors to the carwash bay opened and in I went, rolling through the car wash entrance like Earnhardt in Victory Lane. I was indeed proud of my good fortune. Then it happened, the worst of my carwash nightmares came true.

I somehow went into the carwash entrance and completely missed following the metal tracks that lay before me. I was inside the carwash with tires that seemed to be pointing in every direction. The harder I tried to straighten the vehicle, the farther off-track I became. I think at one point my van was in the carwash sideways. I could barely see for the glare shooting out from the eyes of the people lined up behind me. I think the people in the car two vehicles back were passing out pitchforks and torches.

The carwash attendant came rushing in and begin trying to give me hand signals to help me figure out how to steer my vehicle to the straight and narrow. He stood in front of me and started waving and swinging his hands, arms and fingers and honest to God, I thought he was bringing a C-5 in for a landing. I was now officially doomed. I had no idea what he was trying to tell me to do. Finally, he opened the front door of the carwash and ordered me out. I was then able to back onto the tracks in a more orderly fashion. I'm thankful that this carwash has doors on both ends and I could leave the facility out a door without having to face the people behind me. What a nightmare.

On another note, I was in Laurel last week and went to make a deposit at the bank. I was in a hurry so I used the drive-through teller. I pulled up to one of the teller rows and as usual, I pulled the canister out, placed in my deposit, hit the button and watched the canister shoot up the tunnel into the waiting hands of the teller. As I sat patiently waiting for the canister to return, someone said, "Hello there." I turned to my left and just outside my window, halfway up a poll, was the face of one of the tellers who was inside the bank.

She looked me in the eye and asked how I was doing. I felt like I was in a science-fiction movie. Her face just appeared like Jesus and I must have looked like I just saw the devil because I know my eyes got as big as two manhole covers. I had no idea this type of technology was available here in Sussex County.

All I could think about as I left the bank parking lot was that I was happy I had not been picking my nose or some other hideous thing while waiting for my deposit slip. Oh well, guess we should always be behaving like the whole world is watching anyway.

'Don't make me come up there!'

I think I'm glad that I'm not raising a small child anymore. My son is 19 years old, so for all intent and purposes, he is raised. My patience level has never been good and I think it has gotten worse over the past few years. For this reason alone I would not be good parent fodder at this time.

I do not believe in beating children; that is wrong. However, I would certainly be prone to handing out a "whoopin'" every once in a while as needed. I know there are those who wince when I say this, but I guess I was raised at a time when it was not considered wrong to "burn you up," "bust your bottom," "tan your hide," "blister your rear," "half kill you," or many of the other quaint terms used to describe the carrying out of discipline.

I remember my father was good with a belt. That was his only weapon. He never raised a hand to my brothers or me. He never walked softly and carried a big stick. He just pulled his belt off and meted out justice with preciseness that would be the envy of the Supreme Court. My Dad could be eating a sandwich, unbuckle his belt, "wear us out," and have his belt buckled back up without putting the sandwich down.

We didn't dare run from Dad either; that is unless we could charter a plane to Africa. Even then I would've spent my entire time there watching up in the trees, fearing he would lunge down, swinging by a belt vine like Tarzan. No, we would not run from Dad. Everybody knows that if you run, you get it worse.

My mom was different. She never had any particular tool for carrying out punishments. She used whatever was in her hand at the time. If she was getting dressed and my brothers and I acted up, we might hear a shoe whiz by. If she was doing her hair, it was not unusual to feel a hair brush or comb wrapping across your bare skin. This is why we were as good as gold when she was cutting up cabbage for soup.

My favorite mom-weapon was the yardstick. Mom would be wielding this long, thin piece of paper board as she made contact with our bare legs or arms. I knew it would break before she had struck more than two times, but, I would flail around on the floor screaming as if she was beating me with a piece of lumber.

Mom had a soft heart, so was not long before she was walking away feeling she had "tore me up." When we got older and bigger and mom couldn't handle us as well, she had an annoying habit of hollering at us and nagging us when we were getting on her nerves. We would leave the room with mom right on our trail, still going at it. It made you wish she would just strike us with a shoe and get it over with.

On the other hand, our father was a man of few words. Oftentimes the first thing we heard during our brotherly fights was the swish of the belt as it cut through the air. The first one struck would lunge into a fit of panic, not from pain, but from fright, because he didn't know what struck him.

I guess there are some who feel we were "abused" as children. I disagree. There was also something that was understood about me when I was a teenager, I was stupid. So stupid in fact, that I would challenge my father, this man who spent most of his daily hours wearing a handgun. The fact that my father was a policeman should have given me cause to maintain constant restraint. However, for some ungodly reason, I found it necessary to push Dad over the brink of self-control.

I often defend my father's strict disciplinary rule around my childhood home against those people who call his actions, "child abuse." It is my firm belief that any young'un that is fully aware that his father means business when he threatens retaliation for disrespect and misbehavior, yet continues hell-bent on a mission to challenge that rule, gets everything that is coming to him.

But, it is not as if Dad "picked on me." I really believe wholeheartedly that dad did not have the slightest desire to beat me; he just lived by the "last straw" theory. I always pushed beyond the last straw and on past my father's last raw nerve. When he finally broke from my continuous display of arrogance and ignorance, he would come at me like a medieval warrior.

As young and agile as I may have been, Dad was always several steps ahead of me. When he came at me, belt in tow, it was as if he was moving under a strobe light. I could see his hands clutching the belt and see the belt rise in the air; however, from that point on it was pure Ninja precision. The belt would strike so quickly and in so many different places that I thought Dad had brought along some help.

No, it was not child abuse, it was discipline and I cannot recall any time that I got it that I had not needed it for several weeks. So, in some respects, I guess Dad was more patient than I even gave him credit for.

The 'cowboy' behind the badge

He was the closest thing to a cowboy that I knew of. He walked into the house with his gray, Stetson-style hat and .38-caliber revolver with a leather holster strapped to his side. I loved cowboys when I was growing up. At a young age I considered the likes of Marshal Matt Dillon, Secret Service agent James West, cattleman Rowdy Yates, and the Cartwright boys to be icons. But, where in circa 1960s Crisfield Md. would I find anything close to a cowboy? Actually, it wasn't hard; one lived in my house.

I think my chest must have swollen when I went to school and had the privilege of telling all the other kids that my father was a Maryland State Trooper. Dad was a policeman ever since I was about two years old. I can still remember seeing him pull into the yard in the green and black police cruiser. He would stop the car and then I could see him pick up the police radio microphone and put it to his mouth. I knew he was telling the dispatcher that he was home and off-duty.

He would crawl out of the car with clipboards and papers. His heavy, brown, waist length coat was adorned with badges acknowledging pistol marksmanship, service time, and other notable things. The black belt straps ran around his waist an up on one shoulder. His green slacks were perfectly creased and the black stripe that ran down the side was as straight as an arrow. His black dress shoes were always as shiny as glass.

Dad walked with an air of confidence, no shuffling; simply walking as if each step was meticulously planned. He whistled as he entered the house. I followed him around like a puppy dog. It was exciting to see him hang up his heavy coat and then unbuckle his "six shooter." He would empty the bullets from his revolver and hang the gun and holster at the top of his bedroom closet. It was difficult for me to take my eyes off that gun and holster. It would have been no more appealing to me if it had belonged to Wyatt Earp.

I watched as my father seemed to live out every one of my childhood fantasies. He retired as a state trooper and went on to become chief of police in Crisfield, followed by a term as Sheriff of Somerset County; a lawman in the finest tradition. I guess like most kids at that age, my father was my hero. I loved him, feared him, but most of all respected him. It is amazing how time can allow you to enjoy some of the most precious, inspirational moments, yet if you hang around long enough, you will realize that while you were not looking, time was also stealing from you as well.

My father was 10-feet tall when I was a child. He was the strongest, fastest man in my world. I remember reading in the newspaper about how my father had been involved in a high-speed chase that lasted for almost an hour. He was run off the road and almost crashed a couple times. Then there was the time he chased a suspected car thief on foot through Salisbury. Two Salisbury police officers were stopped at an intersection when they saw this man come running down the street. They thought it was a jogger until they saw my father, full uniform and gun, chasing behind him.

Today my father has become a victim of time. Like all of us, unless we die first, Dad has grown old. Time has taken a lot of Dad's strength and caused him to move a lot slower. He spent the past two weeks in the hospital and I have spent the past two weeks watching him and reliving almost every moment of my childhood. If all goes well, Dad will be going home tomorrow. He won't be wearing his custom fit police uniform and he won't be hanging his gun holster on the nail at the top of the closet. But, now more than ever, I realize that these were only shiny ornaments that adorned the real source of my inspiration: the man behind the gun and badge, my father. Time cannot ever take that away.

Note: Just three weeks after this column ran, my father passed away.

My mother and father before they got married (left) and as I remember them just prior to my father's death.

It was the start of true love

I know that we cannot possibly put a monetary value on the worth of a person. For instance, if you buy a pet, you can usually determine the quality of the animal by the price you paid for it. So, with that in mind, I have often wondered how valuable I must have been to my parents, based on the same formula.

Perhaps if they paid for me by the pound like you would a side of beef, I was quite a prize. But, I figure that some things are better left unknown. However, as luck would have it, I recently had occasion to learn exactly how much my mother and father paid to bring me into the world.

The recent death of my father led my mother to go through packages and parcels from the past. These were things that she had not looked at for decades. Boxes and stacks of paper stuffed inside bureau drawers and behind furniture.

One small, white jewelry box held the secret to my value. As I opened the thin piece of folded white paper there it was in plain English, the exact amount that it cost my mother and father to bring me into the world. I had thought of the thousands and thousands of dollars that must have gone into the birthing process, especially given the costs associated with hospital fees. But, when I looked at the bottom line figure I developed an immediate sense of diminished self-worth. My mom and dad paid exactly $26.47 to the Edward W. McCready Memorial Hospital for me to be brought into this world.

These costs even included the operating room, delivery room services, and five days in the hospital, penicillin and circumcision. If I'm not mistaken, Dad paid more than that for one of his Rhode Island Red roosters. But, I am sure many were the times during my life at home that Mom and Dad felt they had a paid far too much.

Finding the key to my value to the Windsor household was just one of the many treasures that were uncovered in this jewelry box. Probably the most prized find was my mother's diary, which she faithfully kept day by day during her teenage years.

If there is any one thing that can bring true joy into your life, it has to be reading your mother's diary. It is amazing to me that my mother kept track of every day's activities. More amazing is that she was able to capture the day's activities in one sentence. Life was certainly exciting for my mother growing up in Crisfield, Maryland.

I counted 42 passages in which my mother stayed home to "wash my head." I guess in Crisfield, people are less selective and instead of washing their hair like most of us, they washed their entire head. But when Dad came into the picture, I think Mom must have completely forgotten she had a head, because from that day on, there is little reference to staying home at all. They became inseparable. They went to countless carnivals, movies and to each other's homes.

It was easy to tell when Mom was not with Dad because her diary would reflect great desperation. For instance there were few a days in August, 1953 when Dad must have had to do something else, such as eat and sleep, and could not be with Mom.

Diary entry August 25: *"I stayed home tonight. I miss Tom."*

Diary entry August 26: *"I stayed home tonight. I miss Tom."*

Diary entry August 27: *"I went to the movies with Barbara. I miss Tom so bad. Help me, dear God."* Now, that is desperation. But Mom made no bones about her passion for Dad.

Diary entry September 22: *"Tom came down tonight. I need him more than anything in this world."*

Diary entry September 23: *"Tom came down again tonight. I need him now more than ever."*

Diary entry September 28: *"Tom came down after church tonight. I need him more than life."*

There is one entry where Mom must have taken a moment away from her passion and did not go out with Dad. It was Nov. 30, when she had dinner with Dad but stayed home that night because she "got a permanent." I am guessing that had something to do with her head again. But, once again desperation set in because it seems for some reason she did not see Dad the next night and her entry read, *"I stayed home tonight. I miss my man so much. I love him so."*

It is interesting that the last passage in Mom's diary, dated Dec. 31, 1953, states, *"Tom and I went to the movies. I love him so much. He says he loves me. My New Year's resolution: to love Tom forever."*

And guess what? She did.

Epilogue

I wonder where he went?

As I recall he was nothing to write home about in the looks department, but he made up for that with his overwhelming presence. He was not a bad kid, just a child who felt it necessary to garner some sense of attention, even when it resulted in a less than desirable outcome for him, as well as those around him.

Even with all his shortcomings, especially his inability to focus on the job at hand, namely his school work, he was usually well-meaning. I never understood why he found it so necessary to do things that he knew would result in some type of retribution from his father, or a school official. I warned him, but to no avail. It was like he was on a mission to follow through on whatever spontaneous action he felt compelled to do, throwing caution to the wind.

Perhaps his behavior oftentimes left much to be desired. But, whenever I have a few minutes in my busy day to cast my memories back to my childhood, he immediately comes to mind. When I consider the potential he had, I become frustrated that he did not apply himself more than he did.

But there was always something about his carefree, less than structured lifestyle that even today leaves me somewhat envious.

Like most of us, I thought those effortless, devil-may-care days of childhood would never end. As I remember those summers of my youth they all seem to be made up of beautiful, sunny days, with a constant, cool wisp of breeze in the air. The grass seems so green and the dirt under our feet like a soft downy pillow. They are my favorite memories and he was my favorite friend.

No matter what anybody thought, he never meant any harm, even when he was up to no good. I appreciate how he would take me into unchartered territories, pushing the envelope of people's tolerance, even when inside, I was scared about where he was taking us.

The fact is I miss him very much. When I consider the challenges, stresses and deadlines of daily duties and responsibilities, I wonder how he would handle it. I quickly realize that he would not handle it at all; after all, he was just a kid.

I often wonder where he went. I wonder why he left so abruptly, just as life started to become so complicated. I guess he decided that complication was not something he could tolerate. He was more about simple and fun, without the trappings of responsibility, and for that I miss him.

I suppose at this moment he is still running around the yards and streets of Crisfield, making swords, rifles and baseball bats out of old discarded lumber, throwing dirt clods like hand grenades and drinking water from a yard hose or outside spigot. He is running barefoot on the green grass and across the dirt lanes that are as soft as a downy pillow. There is no doubt the sky is blue and the sun bright as the constant cool wisp of a summer breeze blows past his face. I wish I could be there with him as I once was, but that's not possible. So, who was he? He was me.

I do miss the "me" who used to be. Here, at 12, I sit atop the boat that Dad acquired after his brother, Bob, died.

A special acknowledgment: "The Windsor Family"

Again, thanks to my mother and siblings for allowing me to make light of our family and my growing up at home in Crisfield and Marion Station, Md. Pictured are (left to right, standing): younger brother, Jeff, me, and older brother Tom. Kneeling are (left to right): my baby sister, Carol Ann Pankratz, my dear, sweet mother, Frances, and my younger brother, Rob. Missing is the grand patriarch of our family, and my hero, our father, Thomas A. Windsor, Sr.

Thanks for all my wonderful memories!

Thank you so much for reading the book!

We hope you enjoyed "I Think My Dad Was Born in a Barn." We would love for you to check in with us on Facebook and share some of your thoughts and your own life's stories. Visit and "Like" us at:
http://www.facebook.com/IThinkMyDadWasBornInABarn

Made in the USA
Charleston, SC
10 February 2013